Ida's
in the Kitchen

Published by:
Viola Hilltop Publishing, Inc.
1711 Sweetbriar Avenue
Nashville, TN 37219

Author: Ida Ramsey
Cover Art: Charles D. Haston, Sr.
Cover Design: small world productions, inc.
Artwork: Betty Pomarede

Dedication

I want to dedicate this cookbook to my son, Bill Ramsey. He kept urging and encouraging me to compile this book. He deserves all the credit for the publishing and promotion and all the details. I also want to thank my daughter, Betty, for the lovely art work throughout the book. This book is the result of many years of collecting good recipes and trying them in my own kitchen. I want to thank many friends who have been so generous about sharing their excellent recipes with me over the years. I especially want to express my appreciation to Bill's secretary, Jean Moore, for typing all these recipes and for being so patient with my many changes and revisions. I don't have words to adequately express my deep appreciation to Judge Charles Haston for creating and drawing the front cover of this book. It is unique and artistic, and I'm sure he worked on it many hours. Most of all, I want to thank my wonderful family for their patience and encouragement.

I hope that the persons who acquire this cookbook will enjoy cooking and serving these good recipes as much as I have.

Bon Appétit!

Ida Taylor Ramsey

Ramsey- Pomarede

Contents

Memories of the Past

When I came to the village of Viola, Tennessee as a young bride many years ago, I didn't know how to "boil water" as the saying goes. I grew up on a plantation near Como, Mississippi, quite a different place from a farm in Tennessee. My husband, Bob, was very patient with all my mistakes while I was learning to cook. I must have given him a steady diet of bread and toast, because one day he quoted the Bible to me, "Man does not live by bread alone." That did it -- I bought a good basic cookbook. I believe it was a Better Homes and Gardens cookbook. I went exactly by directions in the cookbook. Bob used to laugh and say if it told me to turn around three times I would do it. What really influenced me and inspired me was the superb, delicious food prepared by the ladies around here. I will never forget going to one of those famous Viola picnics when we first married, and eating a piece of Mary Katherine Gaffin's coconut cake. I remember that I had never tasted a cake like that, light, moist, melt in your mouth. She told me that she put coconut in the batter and spooned the milk from the coconut over the cake layers before she covered the whole cake with divinity icing. Besides Mary Katherine's expertise, the light texture was due to "Viola's Best" flour. We used to have a flour mill here in Viola, and they milled flour and meal (grown around here) the likes of which I've never found since. It was a soft wheat flour similar to cake flour, but producing a more moist cake and light as a feather biscuits. I also remember the homemade potato chips; I had never eaten any like that, thin, crisp, and delicious. They told me they had a special slicer to slice them paper thin. Another special treat was the "beef ham." The side of beef was smoked and cured like a pork ham and hung in the smoke house. The taste was almost indescribable, a luscious combination of country ham and steak. From what I can find out, this was unique to this area.

So you can see why I was inspired to compile a cookbook of the prize recipes from the marvelous cooks around here.

My first effort back in the 1940's was the Viola Cookbook, first edition. I had to go around to the persons' homes and ask them for recipes, then write them down. There were many mistakes in this first book. Then a little later when we compiled a second book, I had help from Lib Smartt, Teenie Ramsey and Mary Katherine Gaffin. Many people around here still use this book today. It is out of print, but we did a revised version in 1989.

In 1974, I decided to compile and publish a cookbook of my own in my own handwriting called "Ida Ramsey's Favorite Recipes." In 1978, I decided to write a second book, all different recipes. I have had great success selling these two books; I have sold around 15,000 copies of each book, and they have been a source of much joy to me. So many people write me or tell me how much they enjoy reading and using these books.

I keep on collecting good recipes, so my younger son, Bill, got the idea for me to combine both books, leave out some recipes that were not used as much and add some of the new ones I've collected. All of these recipes have been tried many times by me and by the persons who gave them to me. So I hope this book will be used and enjoyed as much as my other books.

Bon Appétit,

Ida Ramsey

Helpful Hints and Ideas

1. To substitute all-purpose flour for self-rising flour: for 1 cup of all-purpose flour add 1 1/2 teaspoon baking powder and 1/2 teaspoon salt.

2. When starting to bake and you find the raisins have dried out, soak them in warm water before mixing in with the batter.

3. Brown sugar will not harden if an apple slice is placed inside the container.

4. To prevent spattering when pan frying meats, first sprinkle in a little salt.

5. For mock chicken sandwiches, put the contents of 1 can tuna fish in a colander and pour over it 2 cups boiling water. Drain well and flake it. Squeeze a little lemon juice over it. Combine tuna with celery, well-seasoned mayonnaise, chopped peeled apple.

6. For a good, different sandwich filling, mix cottage cheese or cream cheese, nuts, chopped dates and mayonnaise and spread on brown bread.

7. Remember there are two things you have to remember about yeast breads -- temperature has to be even, around 75% to 80%, and you can not rush them. Yeast breads have risen until doubled when you lightly dent with finger and the dent stays.

8. When serving olives on a serving tray, roll olives in olive oil to make them pretty and shiny.

9. When making cakes, always have eggs and milk at room temperature,even cake mixes.

10. A dry cake will result from too much flour, not enough shortening or sugar, too much leavening, over beaten egg whites and over baking.

11. You will have a heavy cake if you use too much shortening, too much sugar, too slow an oven and extreme over beating.

12. To keep nuts and raisins from sinking in a cake, heat them first, roll them in flour, then add to cake batter at the end of mixing.

13. To freeze egg yolks: for 1 cup yolks (barely stir with a fork), mix 2 tablespoons light corn syrup if you are going to use them for making desserts. Use 1 teaspoon salt if you are going to use them for omelets, etc. Put in freezer container and leave 1/2 inch head space. Freeze.

14. Keep marshmallows in freezer. They do not dry out and do not stick when cut with scissors dipped in water.

15. Soak nuts in the shell in salt water overnight before cracking and the kernels will come out whole, and more easily as well.

16. Never store fresh garlic in the refrigerator. Hang up or keep in a little basket.

17. Substitute 1 cup sweet milk plus 1 tablespoon vinegar or lemon juice (let stand 5 minutes) for 1 cup buttermilk (sour milk).

18. Dip frying chicken in buttermilk or let soak in buttermilk, drain, then roll in seasoned flour for crusty, delicious fried chicken.

19. Liver is better if soaked in milk before coating in flour to fry.

20. Store apples with potatoes. It will keep the potatoes from sprouting. Use 1 part apples to 4 parts potatoes.

21. To prevent garlic bulbs from drying out, peel each clove, put in a jar of vegetable oil and cover. The garlic will remain fresh; the oil's flavor will be enhanced for salad dressings.

22. When making coconut cream pies, put the coconut in the chilled baked crust instead of in the filling. The coconut absorbs moisture and keeps the pie crust crisper.

23. If hot fried chicken is not to be eaten immediately, cover with foil and pierce holes in it. The holes will allow steam to escape; the crust will not become soggy.

24. To thicken gravy, sauce or soup, stir instant potatoes into the mixture. No lumps.

25. A fresh coconut in the shell will remain in good condition for a month or more if stored in the refrigerator. To open a fresh coconut, begin by piercing the eyes to drain the milk. Save this liquid to be used to moisten coconut cake. To remove the meat from the shell, bake it in a 350 degree oven for 15 to 20 minutes. Wrap the heated coconut in an old towel to prevent the pieces from flying and tap it with a hammer until the shell cracks. Remove the meat from the broken shell. Peel the inner shell from the meat, then grate with a hand grater or in a food processor.

26. Doughs that rise need an even temperature of about 80 to 85 degrees. You can provide this warm place by setting the dough in an unheated oven with a large pan of hot water beneath it.

Old Remedies and Formulas

Cough Syrup
1/4 cup Bourbon whiskey
1 tablespoon honey
2 teaspoons lemon juice
3 tablespoons pineapple juice

Mix all together and take 2 teaspoons at a time for cough and congestion.

For Stomach Flu
To 1 quart of water add 1 teaspoon of salt, 1/2 teaspoon of baking soda, 4 teaspoons of cream of tartar, and 1 tablespoon of corn syrup. Keeps you from getting dehydrated.

Beef Tea
Take 1/2 pound of lean beef, cut into small bits while raw, put beef into a bottle with very little salt and 1 teaspoon of cold water, place in a kettle of water and let boil one hour. Strain contents of bottle, you will have a very nourishing tea, but too strong for a very weak patient.

Remedy for Bee Stings
Apply a paste made of meat tenderizer and water to stop both pain and swelling.

A Cure for a Chest Cold
One tablespoon each of turpentine, lard, and strong apple vinegar, a pinch of salt, the white of an egg. Shake well and apply externally.

Milk Nog
Break a fresh egg that has been on ice into a bowl with 2 tablespoons of white sugar, beat until light and frothy, then add 1/2 pint of ice cold fresh milk, stir well, grate a little nutmeg and add a little whiskey or rum if desired. Serve at once very cold.

Remedy for Croup
Half a teaspoonful of pulverized alum in a little molasses. One dose seldom fails to give relief. If croup continues, repeat after one hour.

Cure for Warts
Take the juice from a milk weed and apply it to the wart once, and to your surprise it will soon assume a chalk state and will disappear to return no more.

To Keep Away Mosquitoes

A few drops of carbolic acid placed on cotton rags and placed in three or four parts of the room. If in the open air place the preparation near you and the mosquitoes will leave.

For Constipation

Drink a glass of hot water with juice of a lemon before breakfast. It will act as a laxative.

For Arthritis

Juice of one lemon, 8 oz. distilled or spring water, 1 tablespoon real maple syrup, dash of cayenne pepper. Mix and drink 10 glasses a day, no other food for 10 days. On 10th day start eating, salad or steamed vegetables. Relief for arthritis.

For Hoarseness

A small quantity of pulverized borax (size of a pea) dissolved gradually in the mouth and let slowly run down the throat, will stop tickling and cure hoarseness.

Formula for Bubble Bath

1 cup Epsom salt
1/2 cup mild liquid dishwasher detergent
3 to 5 drops of glycerin
3 to 4 drops of perfume

Mix and put 1 to 2 teaspoons under running water to get lots of bubbles.

Hand Cream

1/4 lb. unsalted butter
2 egg yolks
1/2 cup finely ground oatmeal

6 oz. rose water
1 tablespoon honey

Whip together and refrigerate. Rub into hands before retiring.

Silver Cleaner

1 large enamelware pan
1 large piece of aluminum foil
Water to cover silver to be cleaned
1 tablespoon soda to each quart of water used
About 10 minutes of time
1 soft dry cloth

Place foil in large pan. Add silverware (do not overlap). Add water quart by quart. Heat to boiling - remove silver - rinse and polish with soft cloth

Equivalent Chart

A pinch - 1/8 teaspoon or less

3 teaspoons - 1 tablespoon

2 tablespoons - 1/8 cup

4 tablespoons - 1/4 cup

8 tablespoons - 1/2 cup

16 tablespoons - 1 cup

5 tablespoons + 1 tsp. - 1/3 cup

12 tablespoons - 3/4 cup

4 oz. - 1/2 cup

8 oz. - 1 cup

16 oz. - 1 lb.

1 oz. - 2 tablespoons fat or liquid

2 cups - 1 pint

2 pints - 1 quart

1 quart - 4 cups

5/8 cup - 1/2 cup + 2 tablespoons

7/8 cup - 3/4 cup + 2 tablespoons

1 jigger - $1^{1}/_{2}$ fluid oz. (3 tablespoons)

8 to 10 egg whites - 1 cup

12 to 14 egg yolks - 1 cup

1 cup unwhipped cream - 2 cups whipped

1 lb. shredded American cheese - 4 cups

1 lemon - 3 tablespoons juice

1 orange - 1/3 cup juice

1 lb. unshelled walnuts - $1^{1}/_{2}$ to $1^{3}/_{4}$ cups shelled

2 cups fat - 1 lb.

1 lb. butter - 2 cups or 4 sticks

2 cups granulated sugar - 1 lb.

$3^{1}/_{2}$ to 4 cups unsifted powdered sugar - 1 lb.

2 $^{1}/_{4}$ cups packed brown sugar - 1 lb.

4 cups sifted flour - 1 lb.

$4^{1}/_{2}$ cups cake flour - 1 lb.

$3^{1}/_{2}$ cups unsifted whole wheat flour - 1 lb.

4 oz. (1 to $1^{1}/_{4}$ cups) uncooked macaroni

7 oz. spaghetti - 4 cups cooked

4 oz. ($1^{1}/_{2}$ to 2 cups) uncooked noodles - 2 cups cooked

28 saltine crackers - 1 cup crumbs

4 slices bread - 1 cup crumbs

14 square graham crackers - 1 cup crumbs

22 vanilla wafers - 1 cup crumbs

1 tablespoon cornstarch (for thickening) - 2 tbsps. flour

1 cup sour milk - 1 cup sweet milk into which 1 tbsps. vinegar or lemon juice has been stirred

1 square chocolate (1 oz.) - 3 tablespoons cocoa plus 1/2 tablespoon fat

1 tablespoon instant minced onion, dehydrated - 1 small fresh onion

Ramsey-Pomarede

APPETIZERS, DIPS, SANDWICHES

HOT MUSTARD

2 small cans Coleman's dry mustard
3 eggs

1 cup cider vinegar
1 cup sugar

Soak dry mustard and vinegar overnight or several hours. Beat eggs with sugar and add to mustard mix. Cook in top of a double boiler until thick, stirring often.

(Good with ham, use sparingly as it is hot. Keeps well in refrigerator.)

BACON CRACKERS

Nabisco Waverly wafer crackers
Thin sliced bacon
Parmesan cheese

Break block of crackers into separate crackers. Hold each cracker over a bowl and sprinkle with Parmesan cheese. Place half a strip of bacon lengthwise along the wafer, tucking ends under well. Place on rack of large broiler pan near center of oven. Bake at 200 degrees for 2 hours. Do not turn oven up and rush these! Bacon gets very crisp and crackers dry out. (Can be served hot or cold. Can be prepared ahead and stored in tins or frozen. Delicious served with seasoned tomato juice as an appetizer. Men especially like these.)

CRABBIES

1 package of 6 English muffins
l stick margarine or butter
1 can crabmeat, drained well

1 jar of Old English cheese
2 tablespoons mayonnaise
Garlic powder to taste

Soften margarine. Blend well with cheese. Add mayonnaise and garlic powder. Mix well. Blend in crabmeat. Split English muffins into 12 halves. Spread mixture evenly over the 12 halves. Bake at 350 degrees for 10-12 minutes, then broil until golden for 2-3 minutes. Cut into pizza style wedges. Can cut into 6 or 4 pieces each. (These are super for drop-in guests. Can be made ahead and frozen. Freeze on a cookie sheet. When frozen, put into a plastic bag. Let them stand for a few minutes before baking.)

PIMENTO CHEESE SPREAD

1 lb. American Cheese
1 small can evaporated milk (Pet or Carnation)
2 tablespoons vinegar
1/2 teaspoon sugar

1 teaspoon dry mustard
7 ounces pimento peppers

Put cheese and milk in top of double boiler. Let cheese melt. Let cool. Add vinegar, dry mustard, and sugar. Add pimentos, chopped fine. Mix well. Refrigerate. Spread on sandwiches.

CHEESE CRACKERS

1 stick margarine (room temperature)
1 cup plain flour
Dash tabasco
Dash of Worcestershire sauce

1 cup grated sharp cheese
1 cup Rice Krispies cereal

Blend margarine, cheese, and seasonings by hand until thoroughly mixed. Work in Rice Krispies. Pinch off to form tiny balls about the size of a nickel or smaller. Place on ungreased cookie sheet. Press down with a fork. Bake at 325 degrees for about 10 minutes or until light brown. (A favorite at parties.)

EASY CHEESE BALL

2 (8 oz.) pkgs. cream cheese
4 green onions, chopped fine
1 pkg. thin sliced ham, chopped fine
1 tablespoon Worcestershire sauce

Mix all ingredients together well and chill in refrigerator after making into 1 large or 2 smaller balls. Serve with crackers.

Also good for sandwiches.

AVOCADO DIP

Slice a ripe avocado in half. Remove seed and meat but save the peeling halves for serving dip. Put the avocado meat through a blender or food processor to puree.

Combine with:
1 cup sour cream
2 tablespoons lemon juice
Dash of tabasco
1/2 teaspoon garlic salt
1 tablespoon prepared horseradish

Mix until smooth. Put mixture into the avocado peel halves. Place in center of tray with crackers, chips, fritos, etc.

ARTICHOKE DIP

2 cups mayonnaise
2 cans artichoke hearts, minced
2 cups Parmesan cheese

Mix and chill overnight. Put in casserole dish and bake at 350 degrees until bubbly. Sprinkle with paprika. Use as a hot dip with triscuits or chips.

SHRIMP DIP

1 (8 oz.) pkg. cream cheese
2 cups boiled shrimp, finely chopped
1 cup sour cream
1/2 teaspoon Worcestershire sauce
4 or 5 drops of tabasco hot sauce

Salt to taste
2 teaspoons lemon juice

Combine all ingredients. Blend well. Chill for 2 or 3 hours before serving.

DRIED BEEF ROLL

2 (3 oz.) pkgs. cream cheese
2 teaspoons horseradish

6 oz. dried beef

Soften cream cheese, add horseradish and spread mixture on 5 slices of beef, place on top of each other. Roll, wrap in wax paper and chill. Slice just before serving. Serves 6. (Good party food.)

HOT CRAB DIP

8 oz. cream cheese
8 oz. sharp cheddar cheese
1 cup half and half (light cream)
1 can Alaskan crab meat
2 tablespoons Worcestershire sauce

Soften cream cheese to room temperature. Grate cheddar cheese. Melt cheeses with light cream in top of double boiler. Add crabmeat and Worcestershire sauce. Pour into chafing dish and serve <u>warm</u>. Serve with chips or crackers.

HOT BROCCOLI DIP

1 stick butter or margarine
1 can mushroom soup, undiluted
1 pkg. frozen chopped broccoli
1 (4 oz.) can chopped mushrooms (not drained)

1 onion, chopped fine
1 roll of garlic cheese

Melt butter and saute onions until clear. Add soup, mushrooms (with liquid) and cheese until it melts. Add cooked broccoli. Serve hot with Melba rounds, toast triangles or wheat thins. Best served in chafing dish to keep warm. (This dip is different and tasty and really makes a hit at a party or buffet.)

OYSTER CRACKERS

1 (11 oz.) pkg. of oyster crackers
1 small pkg. of Ranch House dressing mix
1 teaspoon dill weed
1/2 cup oil

Mix dry dressing mix, dill weed, and oil in saucepan and let come to a boil. Pour over crackers and toss thoroughly. Bake in a 350° oven in large pan, stirring occasionally. Bake until light brown, about 20 minutes. (Good for snacking.)

RAW VEGETABLE DIP

2 cups cottage cheese
1 pkg. Knorr leek soup mix (dry)
4 tablespoons grated carrot
1 tablespoon chopped parsley

1/2 cup buttermilk
2 radishes, grated fine

Mix cottage cheese and buttermilk in blender (it will be like sour cream but lower in calories). Add other ingredients and refrigerate until ready to use as a dip for raw vegetables. (Raw cauliflower and raw turnips are delicious dipped in this.)

APPLE DIP

1 cup Eagle Brand condensed milk
1 cup butterscotch chips
1 teaspoon cinnamon

Dash of salt
2 teaspoons white vinegar

Melt chips in double boiler. Add rest of ingredients. Refrigerate. To serve take it out early so it will be at room temperature. Serve with wedges of red and green apples (unpeeled). Dip in! (Unusual and good.)

DILL DIP

1 pint mayonnaise
3 tablespoons grated onion
1 teaspoon dried parsley
1/2 tablespoon Lawry's seasoning salt (or to taste)

1 pint sour cream
3 tablespoons dill weed

Mix all ingredients and chill before serving. (Keeps well. Delicious with raw cauliflower, raw squash, celery, carrots, etc.)

CLAM DIP

2 (3 oz.) pkgs. cream cheese
1 teaspoon Worcestershire sauce
Dash of cayenne pepper

1 small can minced clams
4 teaspoons onion juice
Salt to taste

Mash cheese, add all ingredients.
(Delicious served with chips or crackers.)

CHEESE WAFERS

2 sticks butter or margarine
1/2 lb. extra sharp cheese
1 egg white, beaten

2 cups plain flour
1/4 teaspoon red pepper

Grate cheese. Soften butter. Mix all ingredients together except egg white. Use hands to mix together. Roll in small rolls. Wrap in wax paper and refridgerate until chilled. Slice thin into small circles. Place on ungreased baking sheet. Brush top of each wafer with beaten egg white. Bake at 375° for 10 minutes. When almost done, take out of oven and sprinkle with salt. Bake for 5 minutes more. (Nice for a party can make ahead of time).

SANDWICH SPREAD

2 tablespoons butter
1 teaspoon salt
4 tablespoons vinegar

2 tablespoons sugar
2 egg yolks

Cook these ingredients in the top of a double boiler until thick. Remove and add the following:

2 small pkgs. cream cheese
2 tablespoons finely chopped green pepper
1 tablespoon finely chopped onion
1 small can pimentos, chopped
2 cups finely chopped ham or chicken

Spread on thin slices of white or whole wheat bread. (Makes delicious tasty sandwiches for a party or club meeting.)

HAM SPREAD FOR SANDWICHES

4 1/2 oz. can deviled ham
1/4 cup sour cream
2 tablespoons sweet pepper relish
1 teaspoon chopped or grated onion
Dash of tabasco hot sauce

Mix all ingredients together and refrigerate. Spread on small sandwiches.

HAM AND CHEESE SANDWICHES

1 1/2 sticks margarine, melted
2 tablespoons horseradish
2 tablespoons minced onion
1 tablespoon poppy seed
1 tablespoon prepared mustard

Mix all ingredients together and spread on buns. Top with ham and Swiss cheese. Wrap in foil and heat in oven until hot.

CHEESE DREAM SANDWICHES

2 lbs. sharp cheese
1 1/2 cups chopped pecans (optional)
2 green peppers (chopped)
4 tablespoons mayonnaise

1/4 tsp. cayenne pepper
4 ribs celery (chopped)
1 medium onion (chopped)
1 tablespoon
  Worcestershire sauce

Grate cheese and add all ingredients. Mix well and refrigerate. To prepare rolled sandwiches, flatten 1 slice of trimmed bread with a rolling pin. Spread with filling. Roll from one corner of bread to the other. Fasten together with a toothpick. Chill rolls and brush with melted margarine. Toast (not too close to broiling unit) and turn to toast evenly. (These freeze well.) Makes 70. (You can also make these plain, adding seasonings to cheese and omitting celery, peppers and nuts.) (Everyone likes them.)

CHEESE STRAWS

1 lb. grated sharp cheese
1 stick of margarine, softened
2 cups plain four sifted with 1/2 teaspoon red pepper

Work cheese and margarine together with your hands. Add flour gradually working it in well. Let set a while rolled up in wax paper, but do not refrigerate. If you do make it up ahead of time let it come to room temperature before putting it through a cookie press (star design). Squeeze out onto ungreased cookie sheet. Bake at 400 degrees until light brown. These can also be rolled thin and cut out into strips with a pastry wheel. (These are always the hit of a party.)

CHEESE PUFFS

3 oz. cream cheese   *1/2 lb. sharp cheese*
1 stick butter or margarine   *3 egg whites (beaten)*
Red pepper to taste (1/4 to 1/2 tsp.)   *Onion juice to taste*

Freeze unsliced bread, trim, cut into 1 inch cubes. Put cheese mixture in top of double boiler, melt, beat until smooth. Cool. Fold in beaten egg whites. With two forks dip bread into mixture. Refrigerate overnight. Bake in a 350 degree oven for 8 to 10 minutes until slightly brown. Serve at once. (Delicious.)

QUICK AND EASY HORS D'OEUVRES

1.   Wrap oyster in thin slice of bacon and broil.

2.   Sprinkle potato chips with grated Parmesan cheese. Toast in 400 degree oven.

SAUSAGE PINWHEELS

Make your favorite biscuit recipe. Cook sausage (mild or hot as you prefer) until almost done but not hard. Roll out dough and spread with sausage. Roll up like a jelly roll. Chill. When ready to bake, slice fairly thin and put on ungreased baking sheet. Bake at 400 Degrees until brown. Serve hot. (You can freeze these and slice off when you are ready to bake.)

SAUSAGE BALLS

3 cups Bisquick or any biscuit mix
1 lb. hot sausage (raw)]
1 (10 oz.) stick Cracker Barrel cheese (grated)

Mix all together with your hands. Make into small balls (do not pack) and bake on ungreased baking sheet at 350 degrees for about 25 minutes until golden brown. Serve hot. (These make a hit with everyone and are so easy.)

WATER CHESTNUT CANAPE

Slice water chestnuts (3 slices across). Put a dab of mayonnaise on top of each slice. Slice canned shrimp lengthwise, put on top. Fasten together with a toothpick. (A tasty canape.)

CHEESE CORNUCOPIAS

1 1/2 sticks margarine (softened)
1 lb. cheddar cheese (grated)
2 cups plain flour sifted with red pepper (1/4 tsp.).

Mix ingredients well (with hands). Roll out (not too thin) and cut out the size of a silver dollar. Shape (pinching ends together) like flat cornucopias or calla lilies. Insert olive in top. Bake on ungreased baking sheet at 400 degrees until light brown. (Lovely to serve at a party.)

CHEDDAR CHEESE SNACKS

1 stick butter or margarine
1/2 lb. grated cheddar cheese
1 cup plain flour
1/2 pkg. dry onion soup mix

Have margarine and cheese at room temperature. Mix all ingredients together with hands. Shape into 1 inch rolls. Wrap in wax paper, chill. Slice and bake at 375 degrees on ungreased cookie sheet for 10 to 12 minutes.

SHRIMP WHEELS

1 (4 1/2 oz.) can shrimp, drained and mashed
1/4 cup mayonnaise
2 tablespoons chopped stuffed green olives
2 tablespoons chili sauce
1 tablespoon finely chopped celery
1 pkg. refrigerated crescent rolls (8 rolls)

In bowl combine all ingredients except rolls. Unroll dough and separate crescents into 4 rectangles. Spread 1/4 of mixture on each rectangle. Starting at short end, roll up jelly roll fashion. Cut each roll into 10 slices. Place cut side down on greased baking sheet. Bake at 375 degrees for 10-12 minutes. Serve hot. Makes 40. Can be frozen and reheated.

SPICED RIPE OLIVES

Drain 1 pint jar of ripe olives, reserving liquid. To the jar, add 1 small dried chili pepper, 2 cloves crushed garlic, a few sprigs of dill (or dried dill weed), and 3 tablespoons olive oil. Fill jar with reserved liquid and let olives marinate 1 or 3 days before serving. (A tasty hors d'oeuvre.)

CHEESE BALL

1 lb. sharp cheddar cheese, grated
1 (8 oz.) pkg. cream cheese
1 small pkg. Roquefort or Bleu cheese
1/4 teaspoon garlic powder
1 teaspoon Worcestershire sauce
1 small jar stuffed green olives (chopped)

1 small onion, grated
Dash of red pepper
1 teaspoon horseradish
1 cup finely chopped pecans
2 tbl. chopped parsley

Soften cheeses and mix them thoroughly in large bowl of electric mixer. Add all other ingredients except parsley. Mix until smooth, then add parsley. Let chill for a few minutes, then shape into 1 large or 2 smaller balls. Roll in paprika and chili powder mixed. Wrap in foil and keep refrigerated or freeze until needed. Serves about 30. Serve with crackers and let everyone spread their own. (This is always a favorite for open house or informal parties.)

CHILI CON QUESO

2 lb. box of Velveeta cheese
1/4 cup chopped onion
3 jalapeno peppers, chopped

1 pod chopped garlic
2 tablespoons butter
1 can Rotel tomatoes

Melt cheese in top of a double boiler. Saute' onion and garlic in butter. Add to cheese with tomatoes and peppers. (Can add pieces of Monterey Jack or cheddar cheese for flavor. You can add chili without beans to this. Serve with fritos or toasted bread. Serve in a chafing dish.)

CHEESE DATE BALLS

1/2 lb. cheese, grated
1 1/2 cups plain flour
1 pkg. (8 oz.) dates, chopped

1 stick butter or margarine
1/2 cup chopped pecans

Mix grated cheese and butter. Add flour and mix with hands. Roll out a small amount at a time. Cut with small cutter. Fill center with dates and pecans. Shape into balls or crescents. Bake 20 to 25 minutes at 250 degrees until light brown. Roll in powdered sugar. (Different.)

ROASTED PECANS

1/3 stick butter or margarine
1 tablespoon honey
2 dashes of Worcestershire sauce

1 tablespoon vinegar
1 dash hot sauce
4 cups pecan halves

Melt margarine in roaster pan. Mix in other ingredients except pecans. Then stir in pecan halves. Stir well. Roast at 200 degrees for 1 1/2 to 2 hours (uncovered). Stir a few times with a big spoon. Pour out on wax paper, separate and sprinkle with Lawry's seasoned salt. Cool. Store in tins. (Yummy!)

POPPYCOCK

8 cups popped popcorn (1/2 cup of popcorn before popping will make 8
cups after popping)
1 cup roasted peanuts
1 cup toasted pecans

Mix popcorn, peanuts and pecans and keep warm in a greased 9 x 13 inch pan. Sprinkle with salt. Meanwhile, melt 2 sticks margarine, stir in 1 1/3 cups sugar and 1/2 cup white Karo. Cook over medium heat until caramel color (285 degrees) about 15 minutes. Stir often. Add 1 teaspoon vanilla. Drizzle over the popcorn, pecans and peanuts in pan. Take two forks and pull apart. Keep in tins.

GROUND BEEF TURNOVERS

Pastry -
1 cup butter
1 (8 oz.) pkg. cream cheese, softened
2 cups unsifted flour (plain)
1/2 teaspoon salt

Soften butter and cream cheese. Work in flour and salt with your hands into a ball. Refrigerate until ready to roll out. Roll out about 1/8 inch thick and cut out with a 3 inch round cutter. Put 1/2 teaspoon of filling on each round and fold over and crimp edges with a fork. Brush top of each turnover with 1 egg yolk beaten with 2 teaspoons milk or cream. Bake at 350 degrees for 20 to 25 minutes.

Filling -
1/2 lb. ground beef
2 tablespoons chopped onion
1/2 pkg. dry spaghetti sauce mix
1 peeled tomato chopped
1/4 cup water
2 tablespoons grated Parmesan cheese
1/4 cup grated sharp cheddar cheese

Cook the red out of ground beef, add onion and cook. Then add spaghetti sauce mix, tomato and water and simmer for 20 minutes. Remove from heat and add Parmesan and sharp cheese. Cool. Then add 1/2 teaspoon to each pastry round. (These make a hit at a party.)

BACON WRAP-UPS

10 slices bread
15 slices (thin) bacon
1 can mushroom soup (undiluted)
33 toothpicks (approximately)

Trim bread. cut bread into 3 strips. Spread soup thinly on one side. Place half a strip of bacon on underside. Roll up and fasten with a toothpick. Bake on a broiler pan at 300° for 1 hour. Can be made ahead of time. (Tasty!)

CHEESE RING

16 oz. extra sharp cheese, grated
1 cup pecans, chopped fine
3/4 cup mayonnaise or salad dressing
1 small onion, grated
1 clove garlic, pressed or chopped fine
1/2 tsp. tabasco
Dash of worcestershire sauce

Combine all ingredients and press into a lightly oiled ring mold. Refrigerate. Unmold onto a plate when ready to serve. Put strawberry preserves in the center or can use chutney instead of preserves. (This makes a hit at a party.)

HIDDEN VALLEY RANCH PINWHEELS

2 (8 oz.) pkgs. cream cheese, softened
1 pkg. (1 oz.) Ranch dressing mix (original)
1/4 cup mayonnaise or salad dressing
2 green onions, minced
1 (8 oz.) jar diced pimento, drained
Finely chopped broccoli
Finely chopped cauliflower
6-8 12 inch flour tortillas

Mix cream cheese, dressing mix (dry), green onions, and mayonnaise. Spread on tortillas. Mix pimentos, broccoli, and cauliflower. Spread this layer on top of cream cheese. Roll tortillas tightly. Fasten with toothpicks. Chill at least 2 hours. When ready to serve, cut in 1/2 inch pieces. Makes 6 dozen plus. (Great for a party.)

VEGGIE BARS

2 cans Crescent dinner rolls
2 (8 oz.) pkgs. cream cheese
1/4 cup mayonnaise
1 small envelope Ranch dressing mix (dry)
Vegetables - red and green peppers, cauliflower, broccoli, carrots
    (any vegetables you like)
3/4 cup grated cheddar cheese

Spread out rolls on jelly roll pan or large baking sheet. Bake at 350° for 7 or 8 minutes. Let cool. Combine cream cheese, mayonnaise and Ranch dressing mix. Mix until smooth. Spread mixture on top of cooked rolls (flat). Then spread with finely chopped vegetables. Then sprinkle grated cheese over top. Refrigerate for 8 hours. Cut into 1 1/4 inch squares when ready to serve. Makes around 8 dozen. (Different and tasty for a party or buffet.)

Ramsey. Pomarede

Beverages and Soups

VEGETABLE SOUP

Use a large covered cooking pot as this recipe makes several quarts of soup.

*2 1/2 quarts of water (if chicken broth is available use half water and
    half broth)*
A good soup bone
1 beef bouillon cube
1 chicken bouillon cube
2 lbs. lean chopped beef
Salt and pepper to taste

Cook together for 1 hour, boiling gently.

Add:
*   1 large onion, chopped*
*   3 ribs celery, coarsely cut*
*   2 cans (medium) tomatoes*
*   1 pkg. frozen cut okra (use fresh in season)*
*   2 pkgs. frozen lima beans*
*   3 carrots, chopped*
*   3 Irish potatoes, pared and cut in cubes*
*   1 pod red pepper (optional)*
*   1 can tomato soup*

(You can use any left-over vegetables you have) Cook for several hours slowly. If I'm in a hurry and have left-over roast beef and gravy as a base, I add cans of stewed tomatoes and frozen mixed vegetables. You can even use hamburger meat. (Add grated peeled apple to soup about half an hour before serving. It's the magic touch.)

CREAM OF BROCCOLI SOUP

1 pkg. frozen cut broccoli
1 cup half and half (light cream)
1 teaspoon salt
1/2 cup butter
1 teaspoon white pepper
Dash of Worcestershire sauce

3 ribs celery, chopped
4 tablespoons flour
1 medium onion, chopped
3 cups chicken broth
sprinkle of thyme

Cook broccoli in chicken broth until tender. Drain and reserve liquid. Saute' onion and celery in butter until soft. Add flour. Cook for 3 minutes, stirring, but do not brown. Add reserved liquid slowly, stirring all the time. Cook slowly for 15 minutes. Remove from heat and add broccoli and seasonings. Blend in blender or food processor. Add half and half. Return to heat for 5 minutes. Do not allow to boil. (Really delicious.)

SHAKER TOMATO SOUP

1 small onion, chopped fine
1/2 cup celery, chopped fine
2 tablespoons butter or margarine

Saute' these ingredients in margarine until soft.

Add:
1 can tomato soup
1 can water
1 tablespoon lemon juice
1 teaspoon sugar
salt and pepper to taste
1 tablespoon minced parsley

Let simmer for a few minutes. Serve hot with toasted crackers.

SOUR CREAM POTATO SOUP

3 cups raw Irish potatoes, diced
1/2 cup chopped onion
1/2 cup chopped celery
2 teaspoons salt (or to taste)
5 tablespoons butter or margarine
2 or 3 chicken bouillon cubes

2 cups milk (scalded)
4 cups water
1/2 teaspoon pepper
1 tablespoon flour
1 (8 oz.) sour cream

Cook potatoes, onion and celery in water until tender. Add milk, bouillon cubes, salt, pepper and margarine to potato mixture. Blend sour cream and flour until smooth. Add to soup, cook over low heat, stirring constantly until thickened. Simmer but do not boil until ready to serve.

CHICKEN VEGETABLE SOUP

1 small onion, chopped
1 or 2 carrots (chopped or grated)
1 rib celery, chopped
1/2 can of cream of chicken soup
1 cup chunks of chicken (can use canned)
Salt and pepper to taste

1 cup noodles
3 cups water
2 chicken bouillon cubes

Put vegetables, noodles, water and chicken bouillon cubes in a heavy saucepan and let simmer until vegetables are tender. Add cream of chicken soup to thicken. Add seasonings. Then add chopped broccoli, grated zucchini or yellow squash or any vegetables you like. Add chicken. Simmer until vegetables are crisp tender. Serve hot. (Tasty!)

CHICKEN GUMBO

1 (2 1/2 lb.) chicken
1 1/2 lbs. fresh okra (can use
  frozen but fresh is better)
2 tablespoons oil
1/2 cup plain flour
1 large green pepper, chopped
1 lb. andouille sausage, sliced
  (andouille sausage is the delicious
  Louisiana smoked sausage)
1 teaspoon cayenne pepper
1 teaspoon filé powder (optional)

3 quarts water
1/2 cup oil
1 large onion, chopped
2 cloves garlic, minced
1 bay leaf
1 (16 oz.) can tomatoes
1 teaspoon thyme
1 teaspoon basil
1 teaspoon black pepper
2 teaspoons salt
4 cups cooked rice

Cut chicken into 8 pieces, cover with the water, and simmer for approximately 1 hour, until chicken is tender and easily removed from the bones. Pour off stock or broth into large bowl and set aside. Allow chicken to cool, remove meat from bones and set aside. Meanwhile, slice okra and sauté in the 2 tablespoons of oil until all ropiness is gone (about 1/2 hour). In a heavy pot, combine the 1/2 cup oil and 1/2 cup flour. Cook over medium heat, stirring frequently to make a dark brown roux. Add onion, green pepper, celery and garlic and sauté until vegetables are tender. Add sautéed okra, the tomatoes, and sliced andouille sausage. Cook about 15 minutes. Add bay leaf, thyme, basil, pepper and salt. Add the chicken broth, mix well, and bring to a slow boil. Simmer for approximately 1 1/2 hours with the pot loosely covered, stirring occasionally. Add cooked chicken and simmer an additional 15 minutes. Remove from heat, skim off excess fat. Slowly stir in the filé powder. Do not reboil after adding the filé as this tends to make the gumbo stringy. Serve over cooked rice. (This delicious gumbo recipe came from a New Orleans restaurant). (The word "gumbo" is derived from an African word for okra, which is one of the main ingredients of a good seafood gumbo. The dish arrived in New Orleans with the first wave of freed slaves from Haiti, and was immediately taken up by the French Creoles of the city. It has since been a staple of New Orleans cuisine.)

SKINNY DIP SOUP

1 lb. lean ground beef
1 (42 oz.) can V-8 juice
2 cups grated carrots
3 ribs celery, chopped fine
1 medium onion, chopped fine
1 can cream of celery or can of mushroom soup (undiluted) added   last

Cook red out of ground beef in Dutch oven or deep pot. Drain all fat off. Then add V-8 juice, carrots, celery and onion. Simmer for 1 hour, then add celery or mushroom soup (undiluted), stir in and simmer for a few minutes longer. (V-8 juice seasons it, but you can add salt and pepper if you like.) (I grate 1/2 apple on coarse side of grater and add to soup. (Low calorie and delicious)

FRENCH ONION SOUP

2 onions, red or yellow
4 chicken bouillon cubes or
  1 quart chicken stock
1 teaspoon Worcestershire sauce
Small rounds of French bread, toasted
4 tablespoons grated Parmesan cheese

1 tablespoon oil
Cayenne pepper to taste
Salt to taste

Cut onions in rings. Fry very slowly in oil until soft. If bouillon cubes are used, dissolve in 4 cups of water. Mix all ingredients except French bread and cheese. Simmer slowly for 25 minutes. Sprinkle rounds of toast with Parmesan cheese and run under broiler to melt cheese. Place on each serving of soup.

Use crisp crumbled bacon on top of celery, bean or tomato soup.

Croutons are a nice addition to any soup.

CANADIAN CHEESE SOUP

1/4 cup carrots, finely grated
1/4 cup onions, finely grated
1/4 cup celery, finely grated
1/4 cup plus 1 tablespoon flour
1/2 oz. chicken base or 1 chicken
  bouillon cube

1/4 cup butter
1 lb. Velveeta cheese
1 cup hot water
Parsley for garnish

Saute' onions, carrots and celery in butter. Add flour and cook, stirring constantly. Dissolve chicken base or bouillon cube in hot water. Combine with first mixture, add light cream and cheese. Stir together and simmer. Do not let boil. Add parsley for garnish. (A good, hearty soup)

PLANTATION COFFEE PUNCH

1/4 cup sugar
Dash of salt
5 cups whole milk
1 pint vanilla or coffee ice cream
Whipped cream for garnish

1/3 cup instant coffee
1 teaspoon vanilla
Ground nutmeg

Combine sugar, coffee, salt, milk and vanilla. Stir until sugar dissolves. Chill until serving time, then ladle ice cream by large spoonfuls into punch bowl. Pour chilled coffee mixture over this. Top with puffs of whipped cream and sprinkle nutmeg over. Serve in punch cups. 12 servings. (Men like this — different)

GRAPE WINE

2 gallons fruit - crush

2 quarts boiling water

Mix and put in a crock and let stand for 48 hours. Squeeze out juice. Add 1 part sugar and 3 parts juice. Put back in crock and let stand for 6 weeks. Keep in a cool, dry place. Strain and bottle. (A very old recipe.)

HOT TOMATO JUICE

Heat:
- *1 large can tomato juice (24 oz.)*
- *2 cans of beef consomme'*
- *1 can water*
- *1/4 teaspoon tabasco*
- *1 teaspoon prepared mustard (not dry)*
- *2 teaspoons Worcestershire sauce*
- *Dash of lemon juice*

If served in a cup or bowl add 1 thin slice of butter or margarine in each bowl. (Tasty!)

STRAWBERRY PUNCH

1 cup sugar (or to taste)
1 cup boiling water
3 quarts pineapple juice
1 (6 oz.) can frozen concentrated lemonade,
*   dilute according to directions*
1 (6 oz.) can frozen concentrated pink lemonade,
*   diluted according to directions*
1 pint fresh or frozen strawberries, cut
4 quarts ginger ale
8 bottles of 7-up

Combine sugar and boiling water. Stir until sugar is dissolved. Add fruit juices. Chill. Just before serving add strawberries, ginger ale and 7-up. Serve over ice. (You can add a few drops of red food coloring) Serves 75.

FRUITED ICED TEA

8 small tea bags   *1 quart boiling water*
1 cup sugar (or to taste)
1 small (6 oz.) can frozen lemonade (undiluted)
1 small (6 oz.) can frozen limeade (undiluted)
Water to make 1 gallon

Let tea bags steep in boiling water. Remove and add sugar. Add frozen juices and water. Pour over ice.

WEDDING PUNCH

1/2 cup citric acid (may be purchased at a drug store)
8 to 10 cups sugar   *10 quarts water*
2 large cans (24 oz. each) pineapple juice   *Juice of 24 lemons*

Dissolve sugar in water. Add citric acid, lemon, and pineapple juice. Serve cold. Serves around 100 people. (You can add food color in any color you desire or just leave it clear and float a pretty ice ring in the bowl.) (This is a very economical, delicious punch.)

LIME SHERBET PUNCH

1 pkg. lime jello (6 oz.)
1 pint cold water
1 large (24 oz.) can pineapple juice
1/2 gallon lime sherbet

1 pint hot water
Juice of 12 lemons
1 quart ginger ale

Dissolve jello in hot water, add cold water and juices. Add chilled ginger ale and sherbet to juices just before serving. (This punch is a teenager's favorite.)

FROZEN PUNCH

2 small (6 oz. each) frozen concentrated orange juice(dilute according to directions)
2 small (6oz. each) frozen lemonade
1 large can (24oz.) pineapple juice (not frozen)
enough water to finish out 1 gallon   .
sugar to taste (I use 1/2 cup sugar)

Mix all together in large container. Freeze.
Let thaw until just mushy. Just before serving pour 2 or 3 bottles of ginger ale over partially thawed juices at serving time.
(This punch is everyone's favorite-also delicious not frozen.)

GOOD ICED TEA

In a glass container put 6 regular tea bags.
Pour over bags 6 cups boiling water. Cover. Let steep for 5 or 6 minutes. Then add 6 cups cold water. Remove bags, squeezing gently. Add 1 1/2 cups sugar or to taste. Stir well. Let cool and put in refrigerator.

HOT SPICY CIDER

1 gallon apple cider
1/2 cup firmly packed brown sugar
1/2 tsp. nutmeg
20 whole cloves
1 (6 oz.) can frozen orange juice concentrate, undiluted
1/2 cup lemon juice
4 (4 inch) sticks cinnamon

Combine cider, brown sugar, nutmeg, stick cinnamon, and cloves in a large saucepan. Bring to a boil, reduce heat and simmer for 10 minutes. Strain spices from cider. Add orange juice and lemon juice, stir until heated through. Serve hot with stick cinnamon if desired. (16 to 18 servings).

KRIS KRINGLE PUNCH

6 cups chilled cranberry juice
3 cups chilled bottled apple juice
3/4 cup chilled fresh lemon juice
1 1/2 cups chilled orange juice
2 bottles ginger ale (1 pint 12 oz, size)
sugar-if desired

Combine all ingredients in punch bowl. Just before serving pour in ginger ale. Stir well. Garnish with ice ring. Makes 4 1/2 qts.or about 28 servings

Ice Ring: Half fill a ring mold with cold water and freeze until solid. Arrange one or more of the following fruits in a design over the surface of the ice: red and green maraschino cherries, mandarin orange segments, pineapple chunks, lemon or lime slices. Cover with water and freeze. To unmold dip in warm water until loosened. Let float in punch bowl.

COFFEE UKRAINE

1 cup non-dairy coffee creamer
1 cup hot cocoa mix
1 cup instant coffee
3/4 cup sugar
1/2 tsp. cinnamon
3/4 cup sugar
1/4 tsp. nutmeg

Mix all together and store in jars. Measure 3 teaspoons to one mug of boiling water. Can add sugar to taste. (Nice to have on hand to serve guests.)

RASPBERRY SHERBET PUNCH

1 (46 oz.) can pineapple juice
2 bottles ginger ale
3 quarts raspberry sherbet

Mix pineapple juice and raspberry sherbet . Add ginger ale last. Have all ingredients cold. Makes 5 1/2 quarts. (Delicious pink punch).

CREME DEMENTHE PUNCH

1/2 gallon pineapple sherbet
1/2 gallon orange or lime sherbet
3 quarts ginger ale
1 large bottle maraschino cherries and juice (red or green)
1 large can (24 oz.) pineapple juice
2 (12 oz.) cans frozen concentrated orange juice (undiluted)
3 (6 oz.) cans frozen lemonade (undiluted)
1 cup creme deMenthe, green, red, or clear

Mix juices and Creme de Menthe. Add sherbets and ginger ale before serving. (A different, delicious punch).

SPICED TEA MIX

1 large jar of Tang (1 lb. 2 oz.)
1 large pkg. dry lemonade mix
3/4 cup instant tea   2 cups sugar
1 tsp. cloves   2 tsp. cinnamon

Stir all ingredients together and mix well. Put in a jar or coffee can. When you are ready to make tea, put 2 teaspoons of mix to 1 cup of boiling water. (For those who like spiced tea, this is convenient to have on hand.)

APRICOT SLUSH

2 (46 oz.) cans apricot nectar
1 (46 oz.) can pineapple juice
2 (12 oz.) cans frozen orange juice concentrate, thawed and undiluted
1 (12 oz.) can frozen lemonade concentrate, thawed and undiluted
1 (67.6 oz.) bottle ginger ale, chilled

Combine apricot nectar, pineapple juice, orange juice concentrate, and lemonade concentrate in large plastic container, freeze until firm. Remove punch from freezer 1 1/2 hours before serving. Place mixture in a punch bowl, and break into chunks. Add ginger ale, stir until slushy. Yield 8 quarts. (A delicious refreshing punch).

EASY DELICIOUS PUNCH

1 (3 oz.) pkg. strawberry or lime jello
2 cups boiling water
2 (6 oz.) cans frozen lemonade (dilute according to directions on   can)
1 (24 oz.) can pineapple juice
1 quart ginger ale (optional)

Dissolve jello in boiling water. Add lemonade diluted and mixed. Add pineapple juice. Stir thoroughly. Pour over ice in punch bowl. Just before serving add ginger ale. Makes 20 cups. (Can make ice ring or cubes from fruit juice so punch will not be diluted.)

BANANA PUNCH

3 cups sugar
6 cups water
1 large can unsweetened pineapple juice
1 (12 oz.) can frozen orange juice concentrate plus 1 can water
1 (7.2 oz.) can frozen lemon juice concentrate plus 1 cup water
5 ripe bananas, well mashed
3 quarts ginger ale

Boil 3 cups sugar and 6 cups water for 3 minutes. Let syrup cool. Mix pineapple juice, orange juice, lemon juice together for fruit base. Put bananas in blender with some of the juice and mash. Combine cooled syrup and fruit base. Add ginger ale when ready to serve. All but the ginger ale can be frozen, then allow 3 to 4 hours to thaw. Yield 2 1/2 gallons. (This punch is everyone's favorite.)

Ramsay-Pomarede

BREADS

SOUR DOUGH BREAD STARTER

Easy potato starter —

3/4 cup sugar   *1 cup all-purpose flour*
3 tablespoons instant mashed potato flakes   *1 cup warm water*

Mix these four ingredients in glass or ceramic bowl. Cover loosely with wax paper. Let stand at room temperature 2 or 3 days, stirring at least once a day. After 2 or 3 days, the starter will be bubbly and slightly increased in volume. It is now ready to use, or it may be stored in refrigerator in a covered bowl for up to 7 days. After using some of starter, you may keep it going indefinitely in the following manner: Feed by mixing in an additional 3/4 cup sugar, 3 tablespoons instant potato flakes, 1 cup flour and 1 cup warm water. Let replenished starter stand loosely covered at room temperature for 12 hours before storing or using. The part you do not use must be kept refrigerated.

If you do not use and replenish starter at least once a week, discard 1 cup and feed as above to keep active.

SOUR DOUGH BREAD

1 cup easy potato starter   *1 tablespoon salt*
1/4 cup sugar   *1 1/2 cups warm water*
6 cups all purpose or bread flour *1/2 cup oil*

Mix all ingredients thoroughly to make soft dough you can handle. Turn into well greased bowl, turning to get greased all around. Cover loosely with wax paper. Let rise at room temperature 8 to 12 hours or overnight or until double in bulk. Punch down and knead 2 or 3 minutes until smooth and elastic. Dough may be divided into 2 equal parts for 2 loaves or 4 equal parts for 4 small loaves. Pat out in pans and place in greased pans. Let rise for 6-8 hours or until doubled. Bake at 350° for 40 to 45 minutes or until bread is golden brown. Brush each loaf with melted butter then remove from pans onto racks to cool. To make whole wheat bread, substitute 2 cups whole wheat flour for 2 cups of all-purpose flour.

STRAWBERRY BREAD

3 cups all-purpose flour
2 cups sugar
1 tablespoon cinnamon
1 (16 oz.) pkg. frozen strawberries
 (reserve one tablespoon juice for glaze)

1/2 teaspoon salt
1/2 teaspoon soda
4 eggs, beaten
1 1/4 cup oil
1/2 cup chopped pecans

GLAZE: 1 cup powdered sugar
 2 tablespoons lemon juice
 1 tablespoon strawberry juice

Sift together flour, sugar, salt, soda, and cinnamon. Combine eggs and oil. Mix well. Add sifted dry ingredients and mix well. Add strawberries and pecans. Blend until just mixed. Pour into 2 (9 x 5 inch) or 5 (3 x 5 inch) loaf pans that have been greased and floured. Bake at 350° for 45 to 50 minutes or 20 minutes for mini loaves. Pour glaze over warm loaves. Cool. Refrigerate for easy slicing. Freezes well. Delicious with cream cheese spread between slices. Especially good for a party.

TENNESSEE SPOON BREAD

2 1/2 cups milk, scalded
1 cup sifted white plain corn meal
1 1/2 tablespoons butter, melted

1 teaspoon salt
1 teaspoon baking powder
4 eggs, separated

Add scalded milk to corn meal, stirring until smooth. Add salt. Cook in top of a double boiler, stirring constantly until like a thick mush. Stir in melted butter. Cool slightly. Beat egg yolks, add to cooled corn meal mixture with baking powder. Mix well. Fold in stiffly beaten egg whites. Turn into large hot, buttered casserole. Bake at 375° until firm and crust is brown. Serve directly from casserole with a spoon. (This is light as a souffle' and is delicious as a supper dish with fried chicken or ham.) Serves 6 to 8.

QUICK AND EASY CHEESE BREAD

3 1/2 cups Bisquick
1 1/4 cups milk
2 cups (8 oz.) grated sharp cheddar cheese
2 eggs, slightly beaten

Combine Bisquick and cheese, add milk and eggs, mixing until just moistened. Spoon into greased and floured 9 inch x 5 inch loaf pan or in individual loaf pans or muffin tins. Bake at 350° for 50 to 55 minutes for larger loaf pan, less time for individual smaller pans. Remove from pans and serve warm. (You can add 1/2 teaspoon dill weed and 1 teaspoon onion flakes for a different flavor.) (This is so tasty and easy enough for the working gal to make.)

ZOMBIE BREAD

1 lb. sharp cheese
2 sticks (1/2 lb.) melted butter
  or margarine
1/2 cup minced parsley (optional)
2 loaves French bread

Juice of 1 lemon
1/4 teaspoon pepper
1/4 teaspoon garlic
  powder

Melt butter, grate cheese. Mix all ingredients together. Slice almost through 2 loaves of French bread and spread mixture between each slice. Wrap in foil and heat at 325° until hot. (Yummy!)

DILLY BREAD

1 pkg. dry yeast
1/4 cup very warm water (105°)
1 cup creamed cottage cheese (small curd)
1 teaspoon salt
1 tablespoon butter
2 1/2 cups all-purpose flour (more if needed)
1 tablespoon minced onion (or instant onion flakes)
1/4 teaspoon soda

1 egg, unbeaten
2 tablespoons sugar

2 teaspoons dill seed

Soften yeast in warm water with a pinch of sugar. Let stand for 5 minutes. If it bubbles up, yeast is active. Heat cottage cheese until lukewarm. Combine cottage cheese with sugar, onion, butter, dill seed, salt, soda, egg, and yeast mixture. Add flour 1/2 cup at a time, beating well after each addition to form stiff dough. Let rise (covered) 1 hour in warm place. Then stir dough down. Turn into a well greased and floured casserole. (1 1/2 to 2 qt.) or a greased loaf pan. Let rise 45 minutes to 1 hour. Bake in pre-heated 350° oven for 40 to 50 minutes. Brush with melted butter and sprinkle with salt while still warm. (You may also make rolls from this recipe or 6 small individual loaves. (This freezes well. This bread has different, zesty taste.)

DATE NUT BREAD

1 cup dates, pitted
1 1/2 cups boiling water
3 tablespoon shortening
2 3/4 cups plain flour
1 teaspoon cream of tartar
1 teaspoon vanilla

2 eggs
1 1/2 cups sugar
1/2 teaspoon salt
1 teaspoon soda
1 cup nuts, chopped

Cut dates in quarters and pour boiling water over them. Add shortening, sugar, and salt. When cool, add eggs, flour sifted with soda and cream of tartar. Add nuts and vanilla. Spoon into greased loaf pan (can line pan with wax paper greased). Bake at 350° about 1 hour or longer until it tests done but not dry. Cool and turn out of pan. Slice and serve the next day spread with cream cheese or butter. (Really nice to serve at a party or picnic.)

Remember that quick breads are delicious when fresh, but they do not have the keeping qualities of yeast breads.

PUMPKIN BREAD

3 cups sugar
2 teaspoons soda
1 teaspoon baking powder
2 eggs
1/2 teaspoon cinnamon
1/2 teaspoon nutmeg
1 cup raisins (white raisins best)

3/4 cup oil
3 1/2 cups plain flour
1/2 teaspoon salt
1/2 teaspoon cloves
1/2 teaspoon allspice
2 cups pumpkin

Mix sugar, oil, eggs, and pumpkin. Sift dry ingredients together. Reserve a little flour to dredge raisins. Add sifted dry ingredients and raisins. Bake in 3 loaf pans that have been greased (or can line with greased wax paper). Bake at 325° for 50 minutes to 1 hour or until tests done. (This is a spicy, sweet bread — good served sliced and spread with cream cheese.)

ZUCCHINI BREAD

3 eggs
2 cups sugar
2 cups shredded zucchini
1 (8 oz.) can crushed pineapple, drained
1/4 teaspoon baking powder
3/4 teaspoon nutmeg
1 cup chopped nuts

3/4 cup oil
2 teaspoons vanilla
1 teaspoon salt
3 cups all-purpose flour
2 teaspoons soda
1 1/2 teaspoon cinnamon
1 cup raisins

Beat eggs. Add oil, sugar, vanilla, pineapple and zucchini. Add sifted dry ingredients. Coat raisins with flour and add. Add nuts. Pour into 2 greased and floured loaf pans. Bake at 325° for 1 hour or until tests done. Cool in pans for 10 minutes. Turn out of pans on wire racks to cool. (Freezes well.)

QUICK WHOLE WHEAT BREAD

2 1/2 cups whole wheat flour
1/4 teaspoon salt
1 egg, beaten
1/4 cup brown sugar
1 teaspoon grated lemon rind

1/2 teaspoon cinnamon
1 teaspoon soda
1/2 cup molasses
1/4 cup oil
2/3 cup plain yogurt

Sift together dry ingredients. Combine the egg, molasses, sugar, oil and lemon rind and add to dry ingredients alternately with the yogurt. Pour into a greased 9 x 5 inch loaf pan. Bake for 45 to 50 minutes in a 375° oven. May be frozen.

HUSH PUPPIES

1 1/2 cups plain corn meal
2 teaspoons baking powder
2 large eggs
1/2 cup chopped onions

1/2 cup plain flour
2 teaspoons salt
4 tablespoons Wesson oil
1/2 cup milk

Sift dry ingredients into mixing bowl. Stir in remaining ingredients all at once. Drop by teaspoon into deep fat (375°). They are done when they float to the top and turn golden brown. Makes about 4 dozen. (These are very light and crisp and may be kept in sealed jar in refrigerator for a week.) (Delicious with fish.)

GINGERBREAD

2 eggs
1 cup oil
1/2 teaspoon baking powder
1 tablespoon ginger
1 tablespoon cinnamon
1 cup hot water

1 cup sugar
1 cup sorghum molasses
2 cups plain flour
1 tablespoon nutmeg
1 teaspoon soda

Mix together eggs, sugar, oil and molasses. Sift flour, baking powder, and spices. Dissolve soda in hot water. Add dry ingredients and dissolved soda in hot water to egg and sugar mixture. Stir all together. Bake in 9 x 13 inch pan (greased) at 350° for 30 minutes. (Good served with orange or lemon sauce.) (This is a good New Orleans recipe.)

ORANGE SAUCE

1 teaspoon grated orange rind
1 cup powdered sugar

6 tablespoons butter
1 cup orange juice

Mix all together and cook until desired thickness, stirring often. (Especially good served on gingerbread.)

MEXICAN CORN BREAD

1 1/2 cups self-rising corn meal (sifted)
2 whole eggs
2/3 cup oil
2 tablespoons chopped green peppers
1 1/2 cups grated cheese

1 cup buttermilk
1 cup cream style corn
1 chopped hot pepper

Mix all ingredients together except cheese. Pour half of this mixture into a very hot (greased) pan or iron skillet. Sprinkle cheese over mixture, then pour remaining mixture over cheese. Bake at 350° for 45 minutes. Serve hot. (This is tasty, different corn bread.)

CORNBREAD RING

1 cup plain corn meal
1/4 cup sugar
4 teaspoons baking powder
1 teaspoon poultry seasoning
1/4 cup melted shortening

1 cup plain flour
1/2 teaspoon salt
1 egg, beaten
1 cup milk

Sift corn meal and flour before measuring. Then sift dry ingredients together. Beat in egg and milk. Fold in shortening. Pour batter in greased 8 inch ring mold and bake at 425° for 20 to 25 minutes. Serve hot filled with creamed chicken. (A Southern specialty.)

CINNAMON FLOP (HOT BREAD)

4 teaspoons baking powder
1 cup sugar
1 cup milk

2 cups all-purpose flour
1/2 cup shortening
1/2 teaspoon salt

Cream shortening and sugar. Sift together dry ingredients. Add alternately with milk to shortening and sugar. Pour into large greased pan. Sprinkle generously with brown sugar and cinnamon. Dot with butter. Bake at 350° for about 30 minutes. (An old recipe.)

CARROT BREAD

2/3 cup oil
2 eggs
1/4 teaspoon salt
1 teaspoon baking powder
1 cup grated carrots

1 cup sugar
1 1/2 cups plain flour
1 teaspoon soda
1 teaspoon cinnamon
1/2 cup chopped pecans

Cream sugar and oil. Add eggs and beat well. Add sifted dry ingredients. Add carrots and nuts, mixing well. Bake in greased loaf pan (9 x 5 x 2 3/4 inches) in a 350° oven for 40 to 45 minutes.

EASY BANANA BREAD

1 cup self-rising flour
2 eggs
1 tsp. vanilla
1/2 cup nuts, chopped (optional)

1 cup sugar
1/2 cup oil
2 large bananas, mashed

Mix all ingredients together and spoon into greased loaf pan. Bake at 350° for 35 to 40 minutes. (Easy and delicious)

CORN LIGHTBREAD

2 cups plain corn meal
1/2 cup plain flour
1 tsp. dry yeast
2 cup buttermilk

3/4 cup sugar
1 tsp. salt
1/2 tsp. soda
2 tbl. shortening, melted

Sift together corn meal, flour, sugar, soda, and salt. Add dry yeast. Mix well. Add shortening and buttermilk. Stir until just mixed. Bake in greased loaf pan at 375° for 55 to 60 minutes. Let stand for 15 minutes. Turn out of pan. (Good served with ham.) (A very old recipe).

CRANBERRY ORANGE BREAD

juice of 1 orange
coarsely grated peel of 1 orange
2 cups plain flour
1 1/2 tsp. baking powder
1/2 tsp. soda
1 cup fresh, chopped cranberries

1 cup sugar
2 tbl. shortening
1 cup sugar
1 egg, beaten
1/2 tsp. salt
1/2 cup chopped nuts

In measuring cup put juice and rind of 1 orange. Add shortening and enough boiling water to make 2/3 cup. Pour into bowl. Add sifted dry ingredients and egg to orange juice mixture. Flour nuts and cranberries and fold into mixture. Bake in greased loaf pan at 350° for about 1 hour. Test for doneness before removing. Bake at least 24 hours before serving. Slice and serve, spread with cream cheese. (This freezes well. This is a good combination of flavors.)

TINY SHERRY MUFFINS

1 (18 1/2 oz.) yellow cake mix
* 1 (5 1/2 oz.) box instant lemon pudding mix
4 eggs
1/2 cup oil
3/4 cup sherry
1 teaspoon nutmeg
powdered sugar for tops of muffins

Mix all ingredients except powdered sugar in large bowl of mixer. Blend for 5 minutes. Bake in greased tiny muffin tins at 350° for 10-12   10-12 2 minutes or until done. While still warm dip in powdered sugar.

* It's hard to find the 5 1/2 oz. size of pudding mix so I use the small box plus 1/2 of another small box.

Be sure to use cake mix that does not have the pudding in the mix. (These are easily frozen. Lay flat on baking sheets to freeze, then can put in plastic bags. When you defrost them, leave out about 10 minutes, re-heat to serve and dip in powdered sugar.) (Excellent to serve for a party or tea.)

FLUFFY DUMPLINGS

1 1/2 cup plain flour	2/3 tsp. salt
1 tbl. melted shortening or oil	1 egg
4 tsp. baking powder	2/3 cup milk

Sift flour, salt, and baking powder into mixture of beaten egg, milk, and shortening. Drop by teaspoonfuls into boiling chicken broth (about 4 cupfuls), cover and cook gently for 8 to 10 minutes or until done. Serve with baked chicken. (These are light as a feather. An old time recipe.)

BEER BISCUITS

2 cups Bisquick	1/2 cup beer

Mix well. Roll out to 1/4 inch thickness. Cut with small biscuit cutter. Dot with margarine before baking. The yeast in the beer makes the biscuits rise. Bake at 375° for about 15 minutes or until brown. (Very light!)

BANANA ORANGE LOAF

1 1/4 cups sugar	3/4 cup margarine, melted
3 eggs	1 cup mashed bananas
1/3 cup orange juice, fresh or frozen	1/2 tsp. soda
1 1/2 tsp. baking powder	1/2 tsp. salt
2 tsp. orange rind	1/2 cup chopped nuts
2 1/2 cups all-purpose flour	

Cream butter and sugar. Add eggs, one at a time, add sifted dry ingredients alternately with orange juice and bananas. Last stir in nuts and orange rind. Bake in greased and floured loaf pan. Bake at 325° for 1 hour 10 minutes or until it tests done. Cool 15 minutes. Take out of pan.

ICING

1/2 cup powdered sugar	1 tbl. orange juice
dash of salt	

Mix and pour on loaf while warm. Punch holes in loaf so icing will go down into it. (This freezes well and has a delightful flavor.)

SALLY LUNN

1 cup milk
4 cups sifted all-purpose flour, divided
2 teaspoons salt
2 pkgs. dry yeast

1/2 cup shortening
1/4 cup warm water
1/3 cup sugar
3 eggs

Heat milk, shortening and water (120°). Blend 1 1/3 cups flour, salt, sugar and yeast in large mixing bowl. Blend warm liquid into flour mixture. Beat at medium speed for 2 minutes. Gradually add 2/3 cup flour. Add eggs and beat at high speed for 2 minutes. Add remaining flour and mix well. Batter will be thick but not stiff. Cover and let rise in warm place until doubled in bulk (1 hour 15 min..). Beat dough down with a spatula or at low speed of mixer. Turn into greased tube pan (10 inch). Cover and let rise until increased in bulk to 1/2, about 30 minutes. Bake at 350° for 40 to 50 minutes. Serve hot. (This is a very old Southern recipe.)

BEST EVER YEAST ROLLS

2 pkgs. yeast
1 cup warm water (105°)
1/2 cup margarine
2 eggs, beaten
6 to 7 cups all-purpose flour, divided

2/3 cup sugar, divided
1 teaspoon salt
1/2 cup shortening
1 cup boiling water

Dissolve yeast and 1 teaspoon sugar in 1 cup warm water, let stand for 5 minutes. If the yeast bubbles up, the yeast is active. Combine remaining sugar, salt, margarine and shortening in large bowl of mixer. Add boiling water and stir until shortening melts. Cool slightly. Add dissolved yeast and eggs and 3 cups of flour, beating at medium speed until smooth. Gradually stir in enough of remaining flour to make a soft dough. Place in well-greased bowl, turning to grease top. Cover and let rise in warm place until doubled (1 to 1 1/2 hrs.). Punch dough down. Can refrigerate overnight. Turn out on well-floured board and knead several times, adding more flour. Pinch off 2 inch balls and place in greased muffin tins or pans. cover and let rise 30 or 40 minutes. Bake at 350° until light brown. Makes approximately 3 dozen rolls.

POTATO ROLLS

2/3 cup shortening
1 cup mashed potatoes
1 cup milk, scalded
1 pkg. dry yeast
5 cups all-purpose flour

1/2 cup sugar
1 teaspoon salt
2 eggs
1/2 cup warm water

Cream shortening, sugar and salt together. Add mashed potatoes and scalded milk. Let mixture cool. Dissolve yeast in very warm water and a pinch of sugar. Let stand for 5 minutes and if it bubbles up the yeast is active. Add dissolved yeast and eggs to cooled mixture. Mix well. Add 2 cups flour and beat until smooth. Gradually add 2 more cups flour, beating well after each addition. Using hands, work remaining cup of flour into the dough. Turn into greased bowl. Cover with plastic wrap or a towel. Let rise until doubled, then punch down and refrigerate several hours or overnight. When ready to bake, knead in extra flour if necessary, roll out and cut with a biscuit cutter. Fold over and brush with melted butter. Let rise until doubled in size. Bake at 375° until brown. (You can bake these to the browning point, cool, put in plastic bags and freeze.) My favorite rolls — they have a delicious nutty flavor.

HONEY WHEAT BREAD

1 pkg. dry yeast or 1 tablespoon
1/2 cup honey
3 cups whole wheat flour
1 cup milk

2 tablespoons shortening
3 cups all-purpose flour
1 cup warm water
1 tablespoon salt

Soften yeast in warm water (105°) with a pinch of sugar. Let stand for 5 minutes. If it bubbles up the yeast is active. Combine honey, salt, shortening and milk. Stir to melt shortening. Cool to lukewarm. Add softened yeast. Add flour gradually to make stiff dough. Knead on floured surface until smooth and elastic. Place in greased bowl. Grease top of dough. Cover. Let rise until double in size. Punch down, knead and divide into 2 loaves. Roll and fit into well greased loaf pans. Brush with melted margarine or butter. Let rise until double. Bake at 350° about 35 minutes. Brush tops with melted margarine. Turn out of pans on to racks to cool. (The best wheat bread I've ever tasted.)

ANGEL BISCUITS

5 cups unsifted plain flour
1 cup shortening
1 pkg. dry yeast
1 tablespoon baking powder
2 cups buttermilk (room temperature)

1/4 cup sugar
1 teaspoon soda
1 1/4 teaspoon salt
2 tablespoons warm water

Sift dry ingredients together. Dissolve yeast in 2 tablespoons warm water. Add to buttermilk. Cut shortening into dry ingredients. Stir buttermilk-yeast mixture into flour mixture and mix well. Turn out on lightly floured board and add flour if needed for soft dough. Roll out 2/4 inch thick. Cut with biscuit cutter and dip into melted butter and fold over or just leave like biscuits. Bake in preheated 400° oven for 15 minutes. Makes about 5 dozen. Bake without letting rise. The dough may be kept in refrigerator until needed. (These are delicious and nice to have in refrigerator ready to bake. Especially good for a party cut out very small with ham in between.)

SPOON ROLLS

1 pkg. dry yeast
2 cups warm water
4 cups self-rising flour

1/4 cup sugar
1 1/2 sticks margarine
1 egg

Dissolve yeast in water. Add margarine to water after yeast is dissolved. Add sugar, sifted flour. Then add egg and mix well. Batter will be thin. Put in greased muffin tins half full. Bake at 400° for 20 to 25 minutes. (These are so easy and have a different taste. The batter keeps well in refrigerator too.)

SOUR CREAM BISCUITS

2 cups self-rising flour
1 teaspoon water or milk

1 cup sour cream

Sift flour into large bowl. Add sour cream, stir to make soft dough. Add water or milk if necessary. Turn out on a lightly floured surface, knead about 30 seconds. Roll to 1/2 inch thick, cut with floured biscuit cutter. Bake on ungreased baking sheet at 425° for 10 to 15 minutes or until lightly browned. Yield 12 biscuits. (Melt in your mouth.)

QUICK CARAMEL CRESCENT ROLLS

5 tablespoons margarine
3/4 cup brown sugar (packed)
2 (8 oz.) cans Crescent rolls
3 tablespoons margarine, softened

1/4 cup water
1/2 cup pecans, chopped
1/4 cup white sugar
2 teaspoons cinnamon

Preheat over to 375°. In an ungreased 9 x 13 inch pan melt 5 tablespoons margarine. Stir in brown sugar, water, and nuts. Separate each can of rolls into 4 rectangles. Press perforations together to make rectangles. Spread with 3 tablespoons margarine. Combine cinnamon and sugar and sprinkle over dough. Start at short end and roll into a roll. Cut each roll into 4 slices, 32 rolls. Place cut side down in prepared pan. Bake for 20 to 25 minutes until golden. Invert immediately on foil. Serve hot.

SEVEN WEEKS BRAN MUFFINS

1 cup All-Bran (can use Raisin Bran
1 cup boiling water

Set aside and cover.

Sift together:
    2 1/2 cups plain flour
    2 1/2 teaspoons soda
    1 teaspoon salt

Beat 2 eggs, add 1 1/2 cups sugar and 1/2 cup oil. Add to dry ingredients. Stir in 2 cups buttermilk and 2 cups All-Bran. Add 1 cup chopped dates or raisins if you use plain All-Bran. Pour first bran mixture into second mixture. Keep in refrigerator in a large bowl and bake as needed. Bake at 400° in greased muffin tins for 15 to 20 minutes. (These are nice to have on hand.) (Will keep for 7 weeks in refrigerator.)

CINNAMON PINWHEELS

1 pkg. Crescent dinner rolls
(Roll each rectangle thin)

Spread with softened butter, sprinkle with cinnamon sugar, finely chopped nuts and raisins. Roll up tightly. Refrigerate 2 to 3 hours, never overnight. Slice and bake in a 350° oven about 8 minutes. Mix a topping of powdered sugar and orange juice concentrate, undiluted and put a dash on each while pinwheels are still hot. Can freeze and take out as needed.

Ramsey. Pomarede

CAKES AND FROSTINGS

MILK CHOCOLATE CAKE

1/2 cup margarine
1 1/2 squares unsweetened chocolate
1 teaspoon vanilla
2 cups plain flour, sifted with 1/2 teaspoon salt
1 teaspoon soda dissolved in 1 tablespoon vinegar

1 1/2 cups sugar
2 eggs
1 cup buttermilk

Cream margarine and sugar until light. Add eggs, one at a time, beating well. Add melted chocolate and vanilla. Add sifted flour alternately with buttermilk. Last, stir in soda dissolved in vinegar. Bake in two wax paper (greased) lined pans (8 or 9 inch) and bake at 375° for 25 to 30 minutes or until it tests done.

ICING

1 stick margarine
2 squares unsweetened chocolate
6 tablespoons milk or cream

1 box powdered sugar
1 teaspoon vanilla
1 cup chopped nuts
(optional)

Melt margarine and chocolate in top of double boiler or microwave. Put in mixer and beat in powdered sugar, milk and vanilla. Then stir in nuts. Spread between layers and on top of cake. (This cake is easy and delicious).

HONEY BUN CAKE

1 box yellow cake mix
1/2 cup sugar
8 oz. sour cream

4 eggs
3/4 cup oil

Mix all together in large bowl of mixer. Mix well. Then add:

1 cup brown sugar
1 cup raisins

1 cup chopped pecans
1 or 2 tablespoons
cinnamon

Mix well. Pour into greased 9 x 13 inch pan. Bake at 300° for 45 minutes or until tests done. (Cake will sink in the middle.)

GLAZE:
2 cups powdered sugar
1 teaspoon vanilla
5 tablespoons milk

Pour over cake while hot. (Can make into muffins. Very sweet like honey buns.)

EASY SAUCEPAN CHOCOLATE CAKE

2 cups plain flour
1 stick margarine
1 cup water
4 tablespoons cocoa
1 teaspoon soda
1 tablespoon vanilla

2 cups sugar
1/2 cup oil
1/2 teaspoon salt
2 eggs
1/2 cup buttermilk

Preheat oven to 375°. Sift flour, sugar and salt together in large bowl of mixer. In a heavy saucepan put margarine, oil, water and cocoa. Bring this to a boil, then pour over flour, sugar mixture. Beat well. Add eggs, soda dissolved in buttermilk and vanilla. Mix well. Batter will be thin. Bake in a greased 13 x 9 inch pan. Bake for 25 to 30 minutes or until tests done.

CHOCOLATE FROSTING

4 tablespoons cocoa
1 box powdered sugar
1 to 1 1/2 cups chopped nuts

6 tablespoons milk
1 teaspoon vanilla

Mix margarine, cocoa, milk in saucepan. Stir and bring to a boil. Remove from heat and add powdered sugar. Stir well. Add vanilla and nuts. Spread over cake while hot. Cool. Refrigerate. Cut in squares. (Our favorite chocolate cake and so easy).

(NOTE: The new extra moist cake mixes have added oil to the mix, so when you have a recipe using a cake mix as a base, always cut down on the amount of oil. I have done this to the recipes in this book.)

(ALSO NOTE: When testing a cake for doneness with a toothpick or cake tester, it is better to take it out when a few crumbs cling to the tester rather than coming out dry. Then your cake won't be dry.)

GERMAN CHOCOLATE UPSIDE DOWN CAKE

1 German Chocolate cake mix
   with pudding
1 (8 oz.) package cream cheese
1 cup coconut (or more)

1 stick margarine
1 box powdered sugar
2 cups chopped nuts

Preheat oven to 325°. Mix cake as directed. Set aside. Mix cream cheese and margarine in bowl until creamed. Combine with powdered sugar and mix until smooth. In bottom of a greased 10 X 14 inch pan, put pecans on bottom and spread. Then put a layer of coconut. Then pour half of chocolate cake mix over top of coconut. Then pour half of cream cheese mixture over cake, then add remainder of cake mix, then remaining half of cream cheese mixture over the cake. Smooth over top with a spoon. Bake for 45 minutes to 1 hour. Be sure it tests done but not dry. (This is even better than German Chocolate cake made from scratch, absolutely delicious!)

CHOCOLATE CHERRY CAKE

1 box chocolate fudge cake mix   *1 teaspoon almond extract*
1 (21 oz.) can cherry pie filling   *2 eggs*

Dump dry cake mix and rest of ingredients into large bowl; stir by hand until well mixed. Pour into greased and floured 13 x 9 inch pan. Bake at 350° for 25 to 30 minutes. When cake cools, frost with:

1 stick butter   *1 cup sugar*

Melt butter and sugar together. Add 1/3 cup evaporated milk. Bring to a boil and boil for 2 minutes, stirring constantly. Take off and add 1 teaspoon vanilla and 1 (6 oz.) package chocolate chips. Beat until smooth. Spread over cake. (This is moist and delicious - tastes like chocolate covered cherries.)

LEMON LIME REFRIGERATOR SHEET CAKE

1 package (3 oz.) lime jello
1 package Deluxe Lemon Supreme Cake Mix
Topping -
  1 envelope whipped topping mix
  1 package lemon instant pudding
  1 1/2 cups cold milk

Dissolve jello in 3/4 cup boiling water, add 1/2 cup cold water, set aside at room temperature.

Mix cake and bake as directed in greased 13 x 9 x 2 inch pan. Cool cake for 20 to 25 minutes. Poke holes in warm cake with a fork. With a cup, slowly pour jello over cake. Refrigerate.

Topping -   In a chilled bowl, blend whipped topping mix, instant pudding and milk until stiff. Immediately frost cake. Keep refrigerated.

(This is refreshing, especially in summer.)

OVERNIGHT COFFEE CAKE

3/4 cup butter or margarine, softened
1 cups sugar   *2 eggs*
1 (8 oz.) carton sour cream   *1 teaspoon soda*
2 cups all-purpose flour   *1 teaspoon nutmeg*
1 teaspoon baking powder   *1/2 teaspoon salt*
3/4 cup firmly packed brown sugar   *1/2 cup chopped nuts*
1 teaspoon cinnamon

Combine butter and sugar; cream until light and fluffy. Add eggs and sour cream, mixing well. Sift flour, baking powder, soda, salt and nutmeg together. Add to butter, sugar mixture. Pour batter into a greased and floured 9 x 13 inch pan or a Bundt or tube pan. Combine brown sugar, nuts and cinnamon and sprinkle evenly over batter. Cover and chill overnight. Uncover and bake at 350° for 35 to 40 minutes (longer for Bundt or tube pan) or until it tests done. Yield 15 servings.

BETTER THAN SEX CAKE

MAKE ONE TO TWO DAYS BEFORE YOU SERVE IT AND IT IS MUCH BETTER.

Bake one yellow cake mix according to directions on box (I use Duncan Hines Yellow Butter Recipe mix)

Let cool.

Meanwhile, in another very large bowl or pan mix together the following:

Cream 1 - 8 oz. Philadelphia Cream Cheese with two cups sugar. (I let my cream cheese set out till it is room temperature and beat with a hand mixer)
Add
1 - 8 oz. sour cream
1 - 8 oz. Cool Whip
2 - large cans crushed pineapple (drained well)

Stir all this up together slowly.

Half your two cake layers, making four thin layers.

Place one layer on cake plate and gob on icing mixture, adding layers of cake and icing until all icing is gone. Be sure you leave enough to go on top and around sides of cake.

This cake needs to be refrigerated in a cake taker that has a cover on it that seals. Mine is Tupperware's largest cake taker. This is a great summer cake as it is so cool and refreshing.

(This has to be good! This is Jean Moore's recipe — Jean is Bill's secretary and she makes it for him on special occasions.)

APRICOT CAKE

2 cups sugar   *3 eggs*
1 cup oil   *2 cups self-rising flour*
1 teaspoon allspice   *1 teaspoon cinnamon*
1 (7 3/4 oz.) jar of apricot   *1 cup chopped nuts*
  baby food

Combine all ingredients in large bowl of mixer. Mix until blended. Spoon into greased 10 inch tube pan. Bake at 350° for 1 hour or until tests done.

LUSCIOUS ORANGE ICING

Cook to the soft ball stage (240°):

1 tablespoon white corn syrup   *1/2 cup water*
1/8 teaspoon cream of tartar   *1 cup sugar*

Pour the syrup in a slow stream over 2 beaten egg whites. Beat in 1/4 cup powdered sugar, 1 teaspoon orange rind, 1 tablespoon orange juice. Beat the icing until it is the right consistency to spread.

SEA FOAM ICING

2 1/2 cups brown sugar   1/2 cup water

Stir until the sugar is dissolved, then boil without stirring to 238°, the soft ball state. Whip until frothy 2 egg whites and 1/8 teaspoon salt. Pour the syrup over the beaten egg whites in a thin stream. Beat constantly on high speed. Add 1 teaspoon vanilla. Whip until icing will hold a point. Spread on cake.

CREAM CHEESE ICING

Sift 3/4 cup powdered sugar. Beat until soft and fluffy, 2 (3 oz.) packages cream cheese, 1 1/2 tablespoon cream or milk. Beat in sugar gradually. Beat in 1 1/2 teaspoon grated lemon or orange rind or a dash of rum or liqueur.

PRALINE CRUNCH CAKE

1 package (18 1/2 oz.) yellow   1 cup flaked coconut
   cake mix   3/4 cup brown sugar,
1 can (20 oz.) crushed pineapple,   firmly packed
   drained   1/2 cup chopped nuts
1/2 cup butter or margarine, melted

Prepare cake mix as package directs. Pour half of batter into greased and floured 13 x 9 inch baking pan. Spoon half of pineapple over batter. Add remaining batter and top with remaining pineapple. Bake at 350° for 45 minutes. Combine coconut, brown sugar, nuts and butter. Spread over cake. Broil until topping is lightly browned and bubbly. Serve warm or cold. (Easy and good.)

DATE APPLE CAKE

1 1/2 cups oil   2 cups sugar
2 1/2 cups plain flour   1 teaspoon soda
1 teaspoon vanilla   1 teaspoon cinnamon
2 cups chopped, peeled raw apples   1 cup chopped dates
2 teaspoons baking powder   2 eggs
1/2 teaspoon salt   1 teaspoon nutmeg
1 cup chopped nuts

Chop apples after peeling (squeeze a little lemon juice on them to keep them from turning dark), set aside. Measure oil in large bowl of mixer, add sugar and eggs. Beat until creamy on medium speed. Add vanilla. Add sifted dry ingredients (save out 1/2 cup to dredge dates), a little at a time. Batter will be quite stiff. Fold in nuts, apples and dates. Spoon into greased 13 x 9 inch pan or into a Bundt or stem pan. Bake at 350° for 55 to 60 minutes or until tests done. (This is delicious plain or with caramel icing.)

EASY CARAMEL ICING

2 tablespoons evaporated milk
1 cup firmly packed brown sugar

1 stick butter
1/2 teaspoon salt

Heat butter, salt, milk and brown sugar. Stir until sugar dissolves. Add powdered sugar to make right spreading consistency.

RUM CAKE

1 box yellow cake mix
1 (3 3/4 oz.) package vanilla
   instant pudding
1/2 cup rum

1/2 cup water
4 eggs
1/2 cup oil
1 cup chopped nuts

Preheat oven to 325°. Grease and flour stem or Bundt pan and line bottom with wax paper. Sprinkle nuts over bottom. Mix all other ingredients in large bowl of mixer; beat 10 minutes. Pour batter over nuts in pan. Bake for 1 hour or until it tests done. Cool. Invert on serving plate.

GLAZE

Bring to a boil 1 stick of butter, 1 cup sugar, and 1/4 cup water. Boil for 5 minutes. Remove from heat, add 1/3 cup rum. Punch holes in baked cake and slowly spoon mixture over cake. (Luscious! Improves with age.)

YELLOW CAKE

2 cups sugar
3 cups plain flour
1 level teaspoon of cream of
   tartar
1 teaspoon vanilla or lemon flavoring

1 cup sweet milk
1/2 teaspoon salt
3 eggs, separated
1 cup butter
1/2 teaspoon soda

Cream butter and sugar and add egg yolks. Sift together dry ingredients and add alternately with milk. Fold in beaten egg whites and vanilla. Bake in two wax paper lined (greased) 9 inch cake pans at 350°. You can also bake in a 9 x 13 inch pan. Bake for 25 or 30 minutes until tests done. Ice with lemon icing or caramel icing. (Flavor and texture of this cake is wonderful.)

ICING

2 tablespoons butter
1 whole egg, yolk and white beaten
   separately

juice of 1/2 lemon and rind
3 1/2 cups powdered sugar

Cream butter an egg yolks, lemon juice and rind. Beat egg white and add 2 teaspoons powdered sugar. Combine with creamed mixture and stir in remaining powdered sugar. Spread on cake. (You can add yellow food coloring if desired.)

LEMON FILLING

Combine 3/4 cup sugar, 2 tablespoons cornstarch and a dash of salt in a saucepan. Add 3/4 cup water, 2 slightly beaten egg yolks and 3 tablespoons lemon juice. Cook over medium heat until thick, stirring constantly. Remove from heat, add 1 teaspoon grated lemon peel, and 1 tablespoon butter. Cool. (This is delicious between layers of a yellow cake, then ice cake with white icing covered with coconut.)

ORANGE SAUCE

1 cup sugar	2 eggs
2 tablespoons flour	juice and grated rind of 2
1/2 pint whipping cream, whipped	oranges

Cook sugar, flour, eggs and juice of 2 oranges in top of double boiler until thick, stirring often. Cool, stir in orange rind and whipped cream. Refrigerate. (Delicious served on angel food cake.)

MOIST PRUNE CAKE

1 1/2 cups sugar	1 cup oil
3 eggs, beaten	2 cups flour (plain)
1 teaspoon salt	1 teaspoon soda
1 teaspoon cinnamon	1 teaspoon allspice
1 teaspoon nutmeg	1 teaspoon cloves
1 cup buttermilk	1 cup chopped nuts
1 heaping cup of cooked, chopped prunes	1 teaspoon vanilla

Combine sugar and oil; add eggs. Sift dry ingredients together and add to nuts alternately with buttermilk. Blend well. Add vanilla. Mix nuts and prunes and fold into the batter. Spoon into greased and floured tube pan. Bake in a preheated 350° oven for 45 to 50 minutes or until tests done. Can also bake in greased 9 x 13 inch pan or a large loaf pan. Turn tube pan upside down and let cool. Remove from pan and ice with:

BUTTERMILK ICING

1 cup sugar	1/2 cup buttermilk
1 stick margarine	1/2 teaspoon soda
1 teaspoon white corn syrup	1 teaspoon vanilla

Combine all ingredients in heavy saucepan, stirring well. Cook over medium heat until soft ball stage (238°). Cool slightly. Pour over cake. This icing turns brownish and hardens.

PEACH JAM CAKE

3/4 cup butter
1 cup sugar
1 teaspoon soda
   (mix in buttermilk)

1/2 cup buttermilk
3 eggs, beaten separately
2 cups plain flour
1 cup peach preserves

Cream butter and sugar, add egg yolks and beat thoroughly. Alternate flour with buttermilk. Add peach preserves, then fold in beaten egg whites. Bake in two wax paper lined (grease wax paper) 9 inch cake pans. Bake at 350° for 25 to 30 minutes.

ICING

2 cups sugar

1 cup milk

Boil sugar and milk to barely firm ball stage (a little above soft ball on candy thermometer). Stir until cool, then stir in:

1 cup coconut
1 cup crushed pineapple, drained
1 orange (chopped or ground in blender)

1 cup chopped nuts

Put this filling between layers and on top of cake. (This will soak into cake, so it is better the day after baking. This cake is luscious — tastes kinda' like ambrosia.)

CREAMY CARAMEL ICING

2 1/2 cups sugar
1 beaten egg
1 teaspoon vanilla

3/4 cup milk
1 stick butter or margarine

Melt 1/2 cup of the sugar in small iron skillet slowly, until light brown and runny. Mix egg, butter, remaining sugar and milk in a heavy saucepan and cook over low heat until butter melts. Turn heat up to medium (be sure mixture is boiling) and slowly add the browned sugar. Stir constantly all the time and keep on stirring if it lumps some. Cook until it reaches a little above the soft ball stage on candy thermometer. If you test by dropping a little in cold water, be sure you can pick it up into a firm ball. Remove from heat. Let cool slightly. Add vanilla. Beat until right consistency to spread. If it gets too thick, add a little cream. (This will ice a 2 layer cake. This is the best real caramel icing recipe I've ever tried.)

RAW APPLE CAKE

1 1/2 cups sugar
3/4 cup oil
1 1/2 teaspoon soda
1/4 teaspoon nutmeg
1 teaspoon cinnamon
2 cups chopped and peeled raw apples

2 cups plain flour
2 beaten eggs
1 teaspoon salt
1 teaspoon vanilla
raisins, if desired

Mix dry ingredients with apples and raisins. Make a well in the center, add oil, eggs, and vanilla. Spread in a greased 9 x 13 inch pan. Bake at 350° for 30 minutes or until tests done. (Delicious and easy - improves with age.)

CARAMEL FRUIT CAKE

1 lb. dates, cut in pieces
1 cup pecans, chopped
1/4 lb. crystallized cherries, cut
1 can coconut (Angel Flake)
4 slices crystallized pineapple, cut
1/4 teaspoon salt
1 can sweetened condensed milk

Mix all ingredients in large bowl. Mix with hands. Line loaf pan with greased wax paper. Pack in pan firmly. Bake at 300° for 1 hour or until light brown. Cool and wrap in wax paper after removing from pan. Keep in refrigerator. Best to wait a few days before slicing. (This tastes like candy and everyone likes it.)

PECAN PIE CAKE

1 Duncan Hines butter cake mix
4 eggs
1 1/2 cups white Karo syrup

1 stick margarine, melted
1 teaspoon vanilla
2 cups chopped pecans

Blend cake mix, margarine and 1 egg. Save out 2/3 cup of this mixture. Place remainder in a greased 9 x 13 inch pan. To the 2/3 cup mixture, add 3 eggs, Karo, vanilla, and pecans. Mix well and pour over mixture in pan. Bake at 325° for 40 minutes. Cut in squares when cool.

ONE EGG CAKE

1 cup sugar
1 stick butter
2 cups self-rising flour

1 egg
1 teaspoon vanilla
1 cup milk

Cream butter, sugar, egg and vanilla in mixer. Add self-rising flour and milk. Pour into iron skillet (greased brown paper in bottom of skillet). Bake at 350° for 35 to 40 minutes. Turn out and serve warm with a sauce, lemon, orange, caramel or any you desire. (This is a very old recipe and so easy).

EASY COCONUT CAKE

1 small can cream of coconut
1 can Eagle Brand Condensed milk
1 box cake mix (white or yellow)

1 package frozen coconut
1 (8 oz.) carton Cool Whip

Bake cake as directed on box in greased 9 x 13 pan. When cake is done, make holes in cake, then pour cream of coconut and condensed milk mixed together in mixer or blender. Cool, then put Cool Whip and coconut on top. Keep in refrigerator.

SOUR CREAM CAKE

1 stick butter
3 cups sugar
1 carton sour cream (small)
1 teaspoon salt
3 teaspoon vanilla

1/2 cup Crisco
6 eggs, separated
3 cups sifted plain flour
1/4 teaspoon soda

Cream butter and Crisco, add sugar and beat well. Sift dry ingredients together. Add egg yolks, beating well. Add sifted dry ingredients alternately with sour cream. Add vanilla. Spoon into greased tube or Bundt pan. Bake at 300° for 1 1/2 hours. (A wonderful pound cake.)

COCONUT MIST CAKE

3 cups plain flour
2 teaspoons baking powder
1 box powdered sugar
4 eggs, beaten separately
1 cup fresh grated coconut (or frozen)

1 cup milk
1/4 teaspoon salt
1 cup butter
1 teaspoon vanilla

Cream butter and sugar, add egg yolks, beat well. Sift dry ingredients together, add alternately with milk. Add vanilla. Fold in coconut and egg whites (beaten stiff). Spoon into two wax paper lined (greased) 9 inch cake pans. Bake at 350° for 30 to 35 minutes. Can bake in 3 layers. Ice with white icing and sprinkle with fresh grated coconut. (This is the best old-fashioned coconut cake with coconut in the batter.)

WHITE ICING

2 cups sugar
1/4 teaspoon cream of tartar
3 stiffly beaten egg whites

1/2 cup water
1/3 cup powdered sugar
1 teaspoon vanilla

Mix sugar, water and cream of tartar together in heavy saucepan. Stir constantly until it boils. Then do not stir again. Boil (medium heat) until it reaches the hard crack stage (285°-290°). Pour slowly over beaten egg whites in mixer bowl. Beat on high speed. Add vanilla. Then gradually add 1/3 cup powdered sugar, beating well. Spread on cake. (Fluffy and always perfect.)

7-UP POUND CAKE

2 sticks butter or margarine   1/2 cup Crisco
3 cups sugar   5 eggs
3 cups plain flour   1 (7 oz.) bottle 7-Up
1 tsp. lemon flavoring

Cream Crisco and butter with sugar. Add eggs, one at a time, beating well. Add sifted flour alternately with 7-Up. Add flavoring. Beat well. Pour into greased 10 inch tube or Bundt pan. Put cake in cold oven. Turn oven to 350°. Bake for 1 hour and 10 minutes or until tests done. Let cool in pan. Turn out on cake plate. Can bake in two greased loaf pans. (Zippy taste).

POWDERED SUGAR POUND CAKE

3 sticks butter (you can use 2 sticks butter and 1 stick margarine)
2 1/2 cups plain flour (measure before sifting.If you sift before measuring use 3 cups flour)
1 lb. box powdered sugar
6 whole eggs
1 teaspoon vanilla
1 teaspoon lemon extract
1 teaspoon orange extract

Cream butter until light and fluffy in mixer. Add 3 eggs and powdered sugar. Cream well. Then add the other 3 eggs, beating well. Add flour gradually, then flavorings. Beat well for at least six minutes. Spoon batter into two greased loaf pans or 1 large stem or Bundt pan (greased). Bake at 300° for 1 hour or until tests done. Bake longer if you use stem or Bundt pan. (This is our favorite pound cake—the texture is so fine.) (This cake needs no baking powder or soda, because the eggs have leavening power.) (This cake freezes well.) (Any time a recipe calls for flour, it means plain, all-purpose flour. If self-rising flour is to be used the recipe will state self-rising.)

MARBLE CAKE

1 Duncan Hines butter cake mix   4 eggs
1 small carton sour cream   3/4 cup oil
1 package vanilla instant pudding   1 teaspoon vanilla
5 ounce can Hershey's chocolate syrup
1 (6 oz.) package chocolate chips

Mix cake mix, eggs, sour cream, oil, vanilla, and instant vanilla pudding in mixer and beat well. Take half of batter and add 1/2 of the chocolate syrup (save rest for glaze) and the chocolate chips. In Bundt or stem pan that has been greased and floured, put layer of chocolate, then layer of white until batter is used. Run knife through to marbleize. Bake at 350° for about 50 minutes or until tests done. Cool and remove from pan. Make chocolate glaze with rest of chocolate syrup, 1 tablespoon melted butter, and 1 cup powdered sugar, and 1 teaspoon vanilla. Pour or spread on cake. (Easy and delicious!)

WORLD'S BEST CARROT CAKE

1 1/2 cups whole wheat flour
2/3 cup all purpose flour
1/2 teaspoon salt
1 cup brown sugar (packed)
1 cup buttermilk
4 eggs
1 (1 pound) bag carrots, grated
1 (8 ounce) can crushed pineapple
    (drained)
1 cup flaked coconut

2 teaspoons cinnamon
2 teaspoon soda
1/4 teaspoon ginger
1 cup sugar
3/4 cup oil
1 1/2 teaspoon vanilla
1 cup nuts, chopped
1/2 cup raisins

Combine flours, soda, cinnamon, salt, ginger (sifted together). Combine sugars, buttermilk, oil, eggs, and vanilla. Stir until well-blended. Add flour mixture, carrots, pineapple, nuts, coconut, and raisins, stirring just until blended. Grease 3 (8-inch) round cake pans. Line bottoms with wax paper. Bake at 350° for 30 minutes or until tests done.

CREAM CHEESE ICING

1 (8 oz.) package cream cheese, softened
1/2 cup butter or margarine
1 box powdered sugar
2 tablespoons grated orange rind
1 teaspoon orange juice

Cream together cream cheese and butter. Add powdered sugar, orange juice and orange rind. Spread between layers and on top and sides of cake. (This truly is the world's best carrot cake!)

EASY PINEAPPLE CAKE

1 box yellow cake mix. Cook according to directions in a greased 9 x 13 inch pan. Mix 1 large can crushed pineapple with 1-1/2 cups sugar, and 1 tablespoon lemon juice. Stir to dissolve sugar and cook in heavy saucepan for 5 minutes. Set aside. Punch holes in cake with a toothpick. Spoon pineapple sugar mixture on top of cake. Keep spooning it on until all is used. Let set a few minutes.

Frosting:
    8 ounce cream cheese
    1/2 stick margarine, softened
    1 box powdered sugar
    1 teaspoon vanilla

Mix these ingredients together in mixer. Then sprinkle 1 cup chopped nuts over. (Better made the day before.)

APPLE SAUCE FRUIT CAKE

3/4 cup oil
1 package dates, cut
1/2 pound candied cherries, cut
1 cup applesauce
1 teaspoon baking powder
1/2 teaspoon allspice
1/4 teaspoon salt

1 2/3 cups sugar
1 cup nuts, chopped
3 eggs
2 cups flour
1 teaspoon soda
1 teaspoon cinnamon

Cut up dates, nuts, and cherries and add a little flour. Beat eggs, add sugar, oil and applesauce. Add sifted dry ingredients. Stir in fruit and nuts. Bake in greased stem pan or in loaf pans, 1 large and 2 small. Bake at 350° for 45 minutes or until done. (An easy moist cake.)

STRAWBERRY SHORTCAKE

2 cups biscuit mix
1/4 cup butter or margarine, melted
1 beaten egg
4 cups sliced, sugared strawberries

2 tablespoons sugar
2/3 cup light cream
soft butter or margarine
1 cup heavy cream,
   whipped

Mix biscuit mix, sugar, egg, 1/4 cup butter and 2/3 cup light cream well with a fork, then beat vigorously for 30 seconds. Spread dough in greased 8 x 1-1/2 inch round pan. Bake in 450° oven for 15-18 minutes or until done. Remove from pan, cool on a rack 5 minutes. Place on platter. With serrated knife, split in 2 layers, lifting top off carefully. Spread bottom with soft butter. Fill and top with berries and whipped cream. Cut in wedges and serve warm.

EASY CHEESECAKE

1 box yellow cake mix
1 egg, beaten

1 cup pecans, chopped
1 stick butter or margarine

Mix these ingredients with your hands. Press into a 9 x 13 inch pan. Mix well 2 beaten eggs, 8 ounces cream cheese, and 1 box powdered sugar. Pour over bottom layer. Bake at 350° for 30 to 35 minutes. Let cool. (Good with cherry pie filling on top.)

NO BAKE FRUIT CAKE

1/2 pound crystallized cherries
1/2 pound crystallized pineapple
2 pounds pecans, shelled
1 pound marshmallows

1/2 pound dates
1 pound raisins
1 pound graham crackers
1 cup orange juice

Cut up cherries, pineapple, dates and nuts. Roll graham crackers fine. Pour crackers over fruit and nuts. Put orange juice and marshmallows in top of double boiler. Heat and stir until marshmallows are melted. Pour over other ingredients. Mix all together with hands. Line loaf pans with wax paper. Put in refrigerator. Keeps indefinitely. Makes 7-1/2 to 8 pounds. (Very rich and delicious.)

JAM CAKE

1 cup butter
3 cups plain flour
1 teaspoon soda
1 teaspoon each cinnamon, allspice,
    nutmeg
2 cups seedless blackberry jam

1 cup sugar
1 cup buttermilk
4 eggs
1 teaspoon vanilla

Sift dry ingredients together, except soda. Dissolve soda in buttermilk. Cream butter and sugar. Add eggs, one at a time, beating well. Add sifted dry ingredients alternately with buttermilk. Add vanilla and blackberry jam. Bake in two or three layers as you prefer at 350° until tests done.

Filling:
1 cup sugar
3/4 cup milk
1/2 cup chopped nuts
1/2 cup chopped dates
1/2 apple, grated

1 tablespoon flour
1/2 cup butter
1/2 cup coconut
1/2 cup raisins

Mix sugar, flour, add milk and butter. Cook until mixture thickens, stirring occasionally. Remove from heat and stir in nuts, coconut, dates, raisins, and apple. Put this filling between layers. Ice all over with caramel icing. (A good old-fashioned recipe.)

ORANGE SLICE OR GUM DROP CAKE

Sift together 3-1/2 cups plain flour with 1/2 teaspoon salt. Combine 1 pound diced orange slice candy, 1 (1 pound) package pitted dates, chopped, 1 can coconut. Add 1/2 cup of flour mixture, mix well. Cream 1 cup butter, 2 cups sugar, add 4 eggs, one at a time, beating well. Combine 1 teaspoon soda in 1/2 cup buttermilk. Add milk alternately with flour mixture to creamed mixture. Blend after each addition. Add candy mixture, stirring well. Pour into greased and floured tube pan. Grease a piece of heavy brown paper and put in bottom of pan. Bake at 300° for 1 hour and 40 minutes or until it tests done. After removing from oven, pour the following mixture over top while still hot.

1 cup orange juice

2 cups powdered sugar

Cool cake well before removing from pan. (This is a wonderful cake to bake for the holiday season.)

Ramsey-Pomarede

COOKIES, SMALL CAKES, AND CANDIES

SUGAR COOKIES

2 sticks butter
1 cup powdered sugar
2 eggs
1 teaspoon soda
1 teaspoon vanilla

1 cup Wesson oil
1 cup granulated sugar
4 1/2 cups plain flour
1 teaspoon cream of tartar

Mix butter, oil, sugars and eggs. Sift dry ingredients together and add to first mixture at low speed. Add vanilla. Drop in balls the size of a walnut on baking sheet sprayed with Pam. Press balls down with a fork until flat. Bake at 350° for 10 to 12 minutes. (These melt in your mouth! (Taste like Lorna Doone cookies, except better.)

NO BAKE ALMOND BALLS

6 oz. (1 cup) semi-sweet chocolate chips
6 oz. (1 cup) semi-sweet butterscotch chips
3/4 cup powdered sugar
1/2 cup sour cream
1/4 teaspoon salt
1 teaspoon grated lemon peel
1 3/4 cups vanilla wafer crumbs
3/4 cup chopped toasted almonds

Melt chocolate and butterscotch chips together in top of double boiler and remove from heat. Add powdered sugar, sour cream, lemon peel and salt. Mix well. Blend in wafer crumbs. Chill for 15 to 20 minutes. Shape into 1 inch balls and roll in chopped almonds. Yield 3 1/2 dozen. Store in air tight container.

BITE-SIZE FRUIT CAKE

1/4 lb. red candied cherries, cut small
1/4 lb. green candied cherries, cut small
2 cups chopped pecans
6 slices candied pineapple, cut small
1 1/2 cans Angel flake coconut
1 can sweetened condensed milk

1 teaspoon vanilla
1/4 teaspoon salt

Mix all ingredients together. Press mixture together with your hands in bite size cookies. Put on ungreased cookie sheet. Bake at 325° for 10 minutes. Let cool a little before removing from cookie sheet. Makes 5 dozen. (These are colorful and delicious holiday cookies.)

FUDGE COOKIES

1 pkg. (6 oz.) semi-sweet chocolate chips
2 tablespoons butter or margarine
1 cup plain flour
1 can sweetened condensed milk
1 cup chopped nuts
1 teaspoon vanilla

Melt chocolate and butter in top of double boiler or in microwave. Add condensed milk, blend and let stand over heat for 5 minutes. Remove from heat, add remaining ingredients. Drop by teaspoon onto lightly greased baking sheet. Bake at 300° for 10 to 12 minutes. (A children's favorite.)

SAND TARTS OR CRESCENTS

1 lb. butter (no substitute)
6 tablespoons powdered sugar
2 cups ground or finely chopped nuts
2 tablespoons water
4 cups plain flour
1 teaspoon vanilla

Beat butter until creamy. Add powdered sugar and water and beat well. Add 2 cups of the flour and mix well. Add vanilla. Last mix in 2 cups of flour and nuts with your hands. Chill thoroughly. Mold in hands the size of walnuts or in a crescent shape. Bake at 275° for 30 to 40 minutes. Roll in additional powdered sugar while hot. Make 60. (Melt in your mouth.)

FOREVER AMBERS

2 cans sweetened condensed milk
2 cans Angel flake coconut
1 lb. orange slice candy
1 cup chopped pecans
1 teaspoon vanilla
1 teaspoon orange
flavoring

Cut orange slices in small pieces. Mix ingredients together. Spread on heavily greased jelly roll pan. Bake for 30 minutes at 275°-300°. Remove after slightly cooled with teaspoon. Shape with hands into small balls. Keep dipping hands in powdered sugar to keep from sticking. Roll in powdered sugar. Make approximately 7 dozen. (Yummy!)

ORANGE PECANS

1 cup sugar
grated rind of 1 orange
juice of 2 lemons
1 lb. pecans or 4 cups

Cook sugar, juice and rind slowly together for 15 minutes or until it forms a firm ball when tested in cold water (242° on candy thermometer). Drop pecans into mixture while hot and pour out on wax paper. Separate pecans.

APRICOT BARS

2/3 cup dried apricots
1/4 cup granulated sugar
1 1/3 cups sifted plain flour

1 cup brown sugar, firmly packed
1/2 teaspoon vanilla

1/2 cup soft butter
1/4 teaspoon salt
1/2 teaspoon baking
  powder
2 eggs
1/2 cup chopped nuts

Rinse apricots, cover with water and boil 10 minutes. Drain, cool and chop apricots. Set aside. Heat oven to 350°. Grease an 8 x 8 x 2 inch pan. Mix butter, granulated sugar and 1 cup flour until crumbly. Take your hands and press into pan. Bake for 25 minutes. Sift 1/3 cup flour, baking powder and salt. Beat eggs and add brown sugar. Beat until well mixed. Add flour mixture, vanilla, nuts, and apricots to egg-sugar mixture. Spread over baked layer. Bake 30 minutes. Cool in pan.

ICING

1 1/4 cups powdered sugar
2 tablespoons lemon juice

1 tablespoon butter
yellow food color

Mix softened butter, powdered sugar, lemon juice and yellow food color in mixer. Mix until right spreading consistency. You may have to add a little more powdered sugar. Spread on after it cools. Cut into small squares. Makes around 36. (These are always the hit of the party.)

MISSISSIPPI MUD CAKE
or MARSHMALLOW FUDGE SQUARES

2 sticks butter
4 whole eggs
2 cups sugar
1 teaspoon vanilla
2 cups miniature marshmallows

1/2 cup cocoa
1 1/2 cups plain flour
1/4 teaspoon salt
1 1/2 cups nuts, chopped

Melt butter and stir in cocoa and sugar, let cool. Beat eggs and add to cocoa mixture. Sift flour and salt and gradually add to mixture. Add vanilla and nuts. Bake in greased 9 x 13 inch pan in a 350° oven for 25 minutes. Remove from oven and spread marshmallows on top. Return to oven long enough to melt marshmallows. Let cool 5 to 10 minutes. While cake is baking prepare icing.

Icing -
    1/2 stick melted butter
    1/3 cup cocoa
    1/2 cup milk
    1 lb. sifted powdered sugar

Mix in heavy saucepan and let get hot. Pour over so as not to disturb marshmallows. Let cool and cut in squares. (Chocolate lovers love this!)

LEMON SQUARES

1 cup butter   2 cups plain flour
1/2 cup powdered sugar   1/4 teaspoon salt

Mix with hands and pat out flat in a 9 x 13 inch pan. Bake 10 minutes at 350°. Remove from oven and spread with the following:

2 cups sugar   4 eggs, slightly beaten
6 tablespoons lemon juice   1/2 teaspoon salt
4 tablespoons plain flour   1 teaspoon baking powder

Mix these ingredients well. Bake at 350° for 25 to 30 minutes or until golden brown. Cool. Ice with lemon icing:

Lemon Icing -
   2 cups powdered sugar
   1 tablespoon margarine, softened
   3 tablespoons lemon juice
   A little yellow food color

Mix well.

Refrigerate. Then cut into small squares. (Can be frozen. Good party cookie.)

NUT GRAHAMS

1 cup sugar   20 graham crackers
1 cup nuts, finely chopped   2 sticks margarine

Melt margarine and add sugar and bring to slow boil. Add nuts and boil 2 minutes more. Pour over crackers laid out on ungreased cookie sheet. Place the crackers creased side up. Bake at 350° for 10 minutes. While hot, cut on cracker creases. (These are unbelievably delicious and easy.)

HALLOWEEN COOKIES

1 pkg. orange cake mix   2 eggs
1 pkg. (3 oz.) orange jello   1/3 cup milk
1/3 cup oil   6 oz. chocolate chips

Mix all ingredients together and spoon into a greased 9 x 13 inch pan. Bake at 325° for 25 minutes. (Batter will be thick.) Let cool and cut into squares. (Little spooks love these.)

ICED FUDGE SQUARES

1 1/2 sticks butter or margarine
3 oz. (squares) unsweetened chocolate
1/4 teaspoon salt
1 teaspoon vanilla
4 1 oz.) Hershey chocolate bars for icing

4 eggs
2 cups sugar
1 cup plain flour
1 cup pecans, chopped

Melt chocolate and butter in top of double boiler or microwave. Cool. Using a spoon beat eggs lightly, gradually adding sugar, salt, and vanilla. Add cooled chocolate butter mixture. Add sifted flour and salt and nuts. Mix only enough to combine ingredients. Pour into greased 9 x 13 inch pan. Bake at 350° for 25 minutes. Immediately on removing from oven spread chocolate bars all over top. Cut in squares. (You can make this plain without icing.) (This is moist like brownies.)

JEWISH BROWNIES

2 cups sugar
4 1/2 tbl. cocoa
1 1/2 cups plain flour
1 cup chopped nuts

3 sticks butter, melted
1/4 tsp. salt
4 eggs
1 tsp. vanilla

Stir together and spread in greased 9 x 13 inch pan. Bake 20 minutes at 325°. Combine 2 cups coconut, 1 can sweetened condensed milk. Spread over hot cake. Put back in 350° oven and bake 15 more minutes.

FROSTING

3 or 4 tbl. cocoa
1 box powdered sugar
1 tsp. vanilla

2 tbl. melted butter
1/4 to 1/2 cup milk

Mix well and spread on cooled cake.

WORLD'S BEST COOKIE

1 cup butter
1 cup brown sugar, packed
1 cup oil
1 cup crushed corn flakes
1/2 cup ground pecans
1 tsp. soda
1 tsp. salt

1 cup sugar
1 whole egg
1 cup oats
1/2 cup coconut
3 1/2 cups plain flour
1 tbl. vanilla

Combine all ingredients and roll into balls the size of walnuts. Flatten with a fork that has been dipped in cold water. Bake on ungreased cookie sheet for 12 minutes at 325°.

CANDY N' CAKE

Sift together:
  2 cups plain flour
  2 1/2 tsp. baking powder
  1/2 tsp. salt
Cream:
  1/2 cup shortening
  1 cup sugar
Blend in:
  1 egg, beat mixture 1 minute
Combine:
  3/4 cup buttermilk
  1 tsp. vanilla

Add with dry ingredients to creamed mixture

Blend in:
  12 marshmallows, cut into eighths
  1/2 cup chocolate chips

Spread in greased and floured 8 inch square pan.

Combine:
  1/4 cup brown sugar
  2 tbl. butter
  1/2 cup chopped nuts

Sprinkle this mixture over batter. Bake at 350° for 40 to 45 minutes.

ICE BOX COOKIES

3 sticks butter or margarine
1 cup white sugar
1 tsp. soda
2 eggs, beaten
1 tsp. vanilla

1 cup brown sugar, packed
4 1/2 cups plain flour
1 tsp. baking powder
1 cup nuts, chopped

Cream butter and sugars, add eggs and beat well. Add vanilla, then dry ingredients (sifted together) and nuts. Make into small rolls. Wrap in wax paper and refrigerate. Bake as needed. Slice thin and bake at 350° for 10 minutes.

PECAN PRALINES

1 cup light brown sugar, not packed
2 tablespoons butter
2 cups pecan halves
2 tablespoons light corn syrup

1 cup white sugar
1/2 cup evaporated milk
1/8 teaspoon salt
1 teaspoon vanilla

In a heavy saucepan, using a wooden spoon, mix sugars, milk, butter, syrup and salt. Cook to soft ball stage (238°). Remove from heat, add vanilla and nuts. Beat until mixture begins to thicken. Drop by tablespoons on to wax paper. Store in tins.

PECAN PIE SURPRISE BARS

1 box yellow cake mix (reserve 2/3 cups for filling)
1/2 cup butter, melted   1 egg
1 cup chopped nuts

Mix and press into greased 9 x 13 inch pan. Bake at 350° for 15 to 20 minutes.

Prepare filling:
2/3 cup reserved mix
1/2 cup brown sugar, packed   1 1/2 cups dark Karo
3 eggs   1 teaspoon vanilla

Mix all together. Beat at medium speed 1 to 2 minutes. Pour filling over partially baked crust. Sprinkle chopped pecans over. Bake 30 to 35 minutes until filling is set. Cool and cut into bars. Makes 3 dozen.

MYSTERY MACAROONS

1 (5 1/2 to 6 1/4) pkg. buttermilk biscuit mix
1 (2 3/4 oz.) pkg. instant potatoes   1 cup sugar
1 stick melted butter or margarine   1 egg
1/2 teaspoon almond extract   1 teaspoon coconut extract

Mix all ingredients well. Drop from spoon on a non-stick baking sheet. Press with fork. Bake at 350° for 12 minutes. Let cool a few minutes before taking up. (They're good.)

DATE APRICOT BARS

2 eggs   1/4 brown sugar
1/4 cup margarine   1 pkg. yellow cake mix
1 cup dates, cut up   nuts, if desired
1 cup dried apricots, uncooked, cut up   1/4 cup water

Beat eggs, water, margarine and sugar and half of dry cake mix. Stir in other half of cake mix, apricots and dates. Spread in greased jelly roll pan. Bake at 325° for 15 to 20 minutes until light brown. Cool slightly. Spread with lemon glaze.

Lemon Glaze

1 cup powdered sugar
1 teaspoon grated lemon peel
1 teaspoon milk

Add enough lemon juice to make right consistency. Cut into squares and serve.

RUM BALLS

1/2 lb. vanilla wafers (roll into fine crumbs)
1 cup powdered sugar   *2 tablespoons cocoa*
1 cup finely chopped pecans   *1/2 cup white corn syrup*
1/4 cup rum or 1 tablespoon rum flavoring plus water to make 1/4 cup

Mix all ingredients together and shape into 1 inch balls. let set 1 hour. Roll in powdered sugar (additional) and put pecan halves on top. (Good party cookie.)

CREME DeMENTHE SQUARES

1 1/4 cups butter or margarine   *3 1/2 cups powdered sugar*
1/2 cup cocoa   *1 beaten egg*
1 teaspoon vanilla
2 cups graham cracker crumbs
1/2 cup green creme de menthe
1 1/2 cups semi-sweet chocolate chips

Bottom layer: In saucepan combine 1/2 of the butter and the cocoa. Heat and stir until well blended. Remove from heat, add 1/2 cup of the powdered sugar, the egg and vanilla. Stir in graham cracker crumbs. Mix well. Press into bottom of an ungreased 13 x 9 x 2 inch baking pan.

Middle layer: Melt another 1/2 cup of the butter. Combine melted butter and creme de menthe. At low speed of mixture beat in the remaining 3 cups of powdered sugar until smooth. Spread over bottom layer. Chill 1 hour.

Top layer: In small saucepan combine remaining 1/4 cup butter and chocolate chips. Cook and stir over low heat until melted. Spread over middle layer. Chill 1 to 2 hours. Cut in small squares. Store in refrigerator or freezer. Makes 96 small squares.

OATMEAL COOKIES

1 cup brown sugar   *1 cup white sugar*
2 eggs   *1 cup Crisco shortening*
1 1/4 cups plain all-purpose flour   *1 teaspoon cinnamon*
1 teaspoon soda   *1/2 teaspoon salt*
3 cups oatmeal or rolled oats   *1 teaspoon vanilla*
1 cup nuts, chopped (optional)   *1 cup raisins (white or*
                                        dark)

Cream shortening and sugars. Add eggs and beat well. Add vanilla and sifted dry ingredients and oats. Then stir in raisins and nuts. The batter will be so stiff you have to stir last ingredients. Drop by teaspoonfuls on lightly greased cookie sheet. Bake at 350° for 10 to 12 minutes. (You can refrigerate this batter and bake it as you want it.) (One day my youngest son, Bill, came home and said "Mama, I ate some oatmeal cookies that are better than yours." So I had him get this recipe for me. These cookies are addictive — you can't stop eating them.)

CARAMEL LAYER CHOCOLATE SQUARES

14 oz. pkg. (approx. 50) light caramels
1/3 cup Pet evaporated milk
1 pkg. German chocolate cake mix
3/4 cup margarine, melted
1/3 cup Pet milk
1 cup coconut
1 cup chopped pecans
1 (6 oz.) pkg. semi-sweet chocolate chips

In heavy saucepan combine caramels in 1/3 cup Pet milk. Cook over low heat, stirring constantly until melted. Set aside. Grease and flour a 9 x 13 inch pan. In large bowl combine dry cake mix, margarine, 1/3 cup Pet milk and nuts. By hand work dough until it holds together. Press half of dough into pan, reserve remaining for topping. Bake at 350° for 6 minutes. Sprinkle chocolate chips over baked crust, spread caramel over it, then sprinkle coconut over. Crumble reserved dough over top. Return to oven 15 to 18 minutes. Cool slightly, then refrigerate about 30 minutes to set caramel. Cut into 36 bars. (Very rich and yummy!)

PEANUT BLOSSOMS
or HERSHEY KISS COOKIES

1 3/4 cups unsifted all-purpose flour   *1/2 teaspoon salt*
1 teaspoon soda   *1/2 cup sugar*
1/2 cup packed light brown sugar   *1/2 cup shortening*
1/2 cup creamy peanut butter   *1 egg*
2 tablespoons milk   *1 teaspoon vanilla*
48 milk chocolate kisses, unwrapped

In large mixer bowl cream shortening, sugars and peanut butter together. Beat in egg, milk and vanilla. Stir in dry ingredients. Shape into balls (can chill dough first). Roll in granulated sugar. Bake on ungreased baking sheet at 375° for 10 to 12 minutes. Immediately press a chocolate kiss in the center of each cookie. Makes 4 dozen cookies. (Kids love these!) If very thin cookies won't come off the pan, put them back in the oven for a moment and then slide them off.

ENGLISH TOFFEE

1 cup sugar   *1/2 cup butter*
dash of salt   *1 cup almonds*
3 large plain Hershey bars

Melt butter, sugar, salt and nuts together. Let cook until it reaches the hard crack stage (295° - 300°F.) on candy thermometer and is brown. Spread on a baking sheet (not buttered). Cover with candy bars. When melted spread evenly and sprinkle with ground almonds. Break into pieces. (This tastes like Heath bars.)

CHOCOLATE FUDGE

3 cups sugar
3 tablespoons cocoa
6 tablespoons white Karo (corn syrup)
1 teaspoon vanilla

dash of salt
1 cup milk
1/2 stick butter

Mix sugar, cocoa, salt, Karo and milk. Stir constantly until it begins to boil, then do not stir again. Cook to soft ball stage or 240° on candy thermometer. Remove from heat, add butter. Cool for 10 minutes. Add vanilla. Beat until creamy. Add nuts if desired. If it gets too hard, add a little cream. Pour into greased platter or pan. Cut into squares. Store in covered tin container.

Cook candies by stirring them over low heat until sugar is dissolved. Cover the pan for the first 3 minutes of boiling. The steam will prevent crystals from forming on the sides of the pan. Candies made with corn syrup must be cooked to slightly higher temperatures than those made without it.

RIPPLE DIVINITY

3 cups sugar
1/2 cup white Karo
2 egg whites, stiffly beaten
1 cup semi-sweet chocolate chips

1/2 cup water
1 teaspoon vanilla

Combine sugar, water and Karo in a 2 quart saucepan. Stir constantly until it comes to a boil. Reduce heat and do not stir again. Cook until mixture reaches 240° on candy thermometer or until it spins a long thread off the spoon. Slowly pour 1/3 of the mixture over egg whites beating constantly. Cook remaining syrup to 265°, then gradually add to first mixture. Beat until mixture will hold its shape when dropped from a spoon. Add vanilla and fold in chocolate chips. Since mixture is warm the chocolate chips will partially melt and give a rippled appearance. Drop from teaspoon on wax paper. Yield about 4 dozen. (Better than plain divinity — delicious.)

CHERRY DROP COOKIES

3 1/2 cups sifted all-purpose flour
1 teaspoon soda
1 cup butter or margarine
2 cups brown sugar, packed

1/2 teaspoon salt
2 eggs
1 teaspoon vanilla
1/2 cup buttermilk

PEANUT BUTTER FUDGE

2 cups sugar
1 tablespoon butter
2 tablespoons peanut butter
  (crunchy preferred)

1 cup milk
1/4 teaspoon salt
1 teaspoon vanilla

Boil 2 cups sugar, milk and salt and add 1 tablespoon butter while boiling. Cook until it forms a soft ball when tested in cold water. Add peanut butter. Beat until cool. Add vanilla. Pour out on greased pan or platter. Cut in squares.

POPCORN BALLS

2 1/2 quarts popped corn (keep warm)
1/3 cup white corn syrup
1/3 cup water
3/4 teaspoon salt

1 small pkg. peanuts
1 cup sugar
1/4 cup butter
1 teaspoon vanilla

Boil sugar, water, Karo, butter and salt until it spins a long thread when dropped from a spoon or 240° on candy thermometer. Pour over popcorn and add peanuts gradually. Butter hands and shape into balls. (Children love these.)

CHOCOLATE COCONUT CREAMS

2 boxes confectioners sugar
2 cans Angel Flake coconut
1 stick butter or margarine, melted
1 can sweetened condensed milk
1 bar German sweet chocolate
1 (12 oz.) pkg. semi-sweet chocolate chips
1 (6 oz.) pkg. semi-sweet chocolate chips
1/2 cake paraffin
2 cups chopped pecans

Mix condensed milk and coconut and add powdered sugar and melted butter alternately. Mix in nuts. This will be very stiff. Shape into a roll and wrap in wax paper. Leave in refrigerator overnight. Melt chocolate and paraffin over hot water. Slice roll or make into balls. Dip in chocolate paraffin mixture (use tooth picks or candy dipper). Keep over warm water while dipping slices or balls. Place on wax paper and refrigerate to harden. Store in tins. (Can put a maraschino cherry in the center of each ball before dipping.) (Luscious!)

PEANUT BRITTLE

1 1/2 cups raw peanuts
1/2 cup light corn syrup
1 tablespoon butter or margarine
1 teaspoon vanilla extract

1 cup sugar
1/4 teaspoon salt
1 teaspoon soda

Combine peanuts, sugar, corn syrup and salt in large heavy saucepan. Cook over low heat, stirring gently until sugar dissolves. Cover and cook over medium heat 2 to 3 minutes to wash down sugar crystals from sides of pan. Uncover and cook, stirring occasionally to hard crack stage (300°). Stir in butter, soda and vanilla. Pour into a buttered 15 x 10 x 1 inch jelly roll pan, spreading thinly. Let cool. Break into pieces. Yield about 1 lb.

Microwave Directions: Combine sugar, corn syrup, peanuts and salt in a 2 quart casserole, stir well. Microwave on high 8 to 10 minutes. Mixture will be light brown in color. Add butter and vanilla. Blend thoroughly. Microwave on high 1 to 3 minutes or until mixture reaches the hard crack stage (300°). Stir in soda quickly. Pour onto greased slab or cookie sheet. Let cool at least 1 hour. Break into small pieces. Store in air tight container.

PEANUT BUTTER BALLS

2 sticks butter or margarine
1/2 cup smooth peanut butter
1/2 cup chopped nuts
1 (6 oz.) pkg. chocolate chips
1/4 stick paraffin

1 1/2 cups oatmeal
1 lb. powdered sugar
1 cup coconut
1/2 cup raisins
1 teaspoon vanilla

Melt chocolate chips and paraffin. Mix all other ingredients together and shape with hands into balls. Dip each ball in melted chocolate. (Use a spoon or toothpick to dip balls.) Let chocolate drip off and place on wax paper to dry. Refrigerate. When chocolate hardens, store in tins. (Easy and good. A favorite with children.)

NUTTY WHITE FUDGE

2 cups sugar
2/3 cup light corn syrup
2 tablespoons butter
2 teaspoons vanilla

1/2 cup sour cream
1/8 teaspoon salt
1 cup chopped nuts

Combine sugar, salt, sour cream, corn syrup and butter in heavy saucepan. Stir to dissolve sugar. Bring to a boil. Cover and boil for 3 minutes. Uncover and cook until mixture reaches 238° on candy thermometer. Add pecans and vanilla. Beat until fudge gets thick and begins to lose its gloss. Pour into buttered 8 inch square pan. Makes 2 dozen pieces.

DESSERTS

PRALINE ICE CREAM SAUCE

1 cup firmly packed light brown sugar
1/4 cup light corn syrup
1/2 cup half and half (light cream)
2 tablespoons butter or margarine

1/8 teaspoon salt
1 teaspoon vanilla
1 cup pecan halves
vanilla ice cream

Combine all ingredients except ice cream in a saucepan. Cook over medium heat, stirring constantly for 10 minutes or until sauce is thickened and smooth. Cool slightly, serve over vanilla ice cream. Yield 1 1/2 cups. (This sauce may be stored in a covered container in the refrigerator for several days. Before serving, add a small amount of cream, then heat, stirring until smooth. (Lots of calories, but oh, so good!)

FOUR LAYER DELIGHT

1st layer - 1 cup plain flour, 1 stick margarine, 1/2 cup finely chopped nuts.

Mix and press with hands into 9 x 13 inch pan.
Bake at 350° for 20 minutes.

2nd layer - 1 (8 oz.) pkg. cream cheese, 1 cup powdered sugar, 1 cup Cool Whip (from 9 oz. size)

Mix and put on top of first layer after it has cooled. Sprinkle with toasted coconut.

3rd layer - 2 boxes instant coconut cram pie filling mixed with 3 cups milk.

Pour over second layer.

4th layer - top with remaining Cool Whip and toasted coconut and 1 cup chopped pecans.

Refrigerate. (A truly delicious dessert.)

HARD SAUCE

1/2 lb. butter
1 lb. box powdered sugar

1/4 cup cream

Cream butter well, add sugar and cream. Flavor to taste with whiskey or flavoring to suit taste. Chill until firm. (Good on plum pudding or fruit cake.)

CHOCOLATE PEANUT DESSERT

Make a vanilla wafer crust —

1 1/2 cups vanilla wafer crumbs, 6 tablespoons melted butter. Mix and press into a 9 x 13 inch pyrex or pan. Soften 1/2 gallon of chocolate ice cream. Mix 1 cup of nutty peanut butter and 8 oz. Cool Whip into ice cream with a potato masher.

Spread on crust - freeze.

FROZEN PEPPERMINT DESSERT

1 cup vanilla wafer crumbs	2/3 cup margarine
2 squares chocolate (unsweetened)	2 cups powdered sugar
2 eggs, separated	1 teaspoon vanilla
1/2 gal. peppermint ice cream	1/2 cup chopped pecans

In an ungreased 9 x 13 inch pan, spread 3/4 cup vanilla wafer crumbs. Melt chocolate and margarine, add powdered sugar, egg yolks, vanilla and nuts. Mix well, then fold in stiffly beaten egg whites. Spread over crumbs and freeze for two hours. Soften ice cream and spread over chocolate. Top with remaining crumbs. Freeze at least 8 hours. To serve top with chocolate sauce.

CHOCOLATE SAUCE

1 stick margarine	2 cups powdered sugar
1 small pkg. (6 oz.) chocolate chips	1 1/3 cups evaporated milk

Melt margarine and chocolate chips. Add sugar and evaporated milk. Boil 8 minutes, stirring all the time on low heat. This mixture becomes very thick. It will keep in refrigerator, just warm to serve.

ALMOND DELIGHT

1/4 cup brown sugar	1 stick margarine
1 small pkg. sliced almonds	1 can Angel Flake coconut
1 cup all-purpose plain flour	

Mix these ingredients together with hands and pat out in a 9 x 13 inch pan. Bake at 350° for 20 to 25 minutes, stirring every few minutes. Cool. Take out a little less than half and pat remaining down in pan. Beat 2 small pkgs. of vanilla instant pudding with 2 2/3 cups milk and fold in a 9 oz. container of Cool Whip. Spread on baked layer in pan. Sprinkle the rest of mixture you took out on top. Sprinkle additional sliced almonds on top if desired. Refrigerate. Serves 16. (This is a luscious dessert — always makes a hit!)

DESSERT SAUCE OR TOPPING

1 can sweetened condensed milk	1/3 cup fresh lemon juice
1 tablespoon grated lemon rind	2 cups sour cream

Blend milk, lemon juice and rind together. Fold in sour cream. Chill in refrigerator. Delicious over fresh fruit. (Easy, quick, delicious!)

VANILLA ICE CREAM

6 whole eggs
3 pints whipping cream
5 cups milk (or more)

2 1/2 cups sugar
3 tablespoons vanilla

Beat eggs and sugar well in mixer. Add cream and vanilla. Pour into a gallon ice cream freezer and add milk to 3/4 of top. Freeze. (This is the easiest, best ice cream!)

HAWAIIAN PUDDING

3 bananas, sliced
1 can sweetened condensed milk
1 small can (8 1/4 oz.) crushed
    pineapple, drained
1 large carton Cool Whip

3 tablespoons sugar
1 cup flaked coconut
1 cup pecans, chopped
juice of 3 lemons
Maraschino cherries

Mix condensed milk, sugar and lemon juice. Add sliced bananas, pineapple, coconut and pecans and mix together. Pour into 9 x 13 inch pyrex dish. Spread with topping and refrigerate. Dot with cherries before serving.

FROZEN STRAWBERRY DESSERT

1 cup sifted plain flour
1 stick butter or margarine, melted

1/4 cup brown sugar
1/2 cup chopped pecans

Work together above ingredients with hands. Pat out evenly in shallow baking pan. Bake at 325° for 20 minutes, stirring several times. Sprinkle 2/3 of this mixture in 9 x 13 inch pyrex dish. Reserve the rest for later.

2 teaspoons lemon juice
1 cup sugar
2 cups sliced strawberries or
    10 oz. frozen berries
    (cut down amount of sugar if you use frozen berries)
2 egg whites, unbeaten
1/2 pint cream before whipped

Combine lemon juice, sugar, berries and unbeaten egg whites in large bowl of mixer. Beat at medium speed for 10 minutes. Fold in whipped cream. Spread on the crumbs in pyrex dish. Top with remaining crumbs. Freeze.

APPLE STRUDEL

Make pastry and roll out in a rectangle or triangle. Put 2 cups finely chopped apples in center and sprinkle cinnamon and nutmeg on apples. Fold up tight and seal ends. Lay in long baking dish in which 1 stick melted butter or margarine has been put in. Cut 1 inch cuts in top. Mix 2 cups sugar with 2 cups water. Heat until sugar is dissolved. Cool. Pour over pastry apple roll. Bake at 350° for 45 minutes. Baste twice during baking. (Luscious!)

APRICOT NECTAR DESSERT

1 large round angel food cake (10 inch)
1 quart apricot nectar (2 (12 oz.) cans)
1 1/2 cups sugar   7 tablespoons cornstarch
1 tablespoon plain gelatin   1/2 pint whipping cream

Break cake into small pieces and place in large 9 x 13 inch pyrex dish. Combine in a saucepan the apricot nectar, sugar, cornstarch and gelatin. Cook until thickened, stirring constantly. While hot, pour over cake and let stand all night in refrigerator. The sauce makes a marbled effect as it seeps through the pieces of cake. Whip cream and pour over cake. Cut into squares to serve. Serves 12-15.

PINEAPPLE ICE BOX DESSERT

1 package jiffy cake mix (yellow)

Bake by directions on box except use 1/2 cup pineapple juice instead of water called for on box. Bake in greased 9 x 13 inch pan. After cake cools make 1 (5 1/4 oz.) box of instant vanilla pudding by directions on box. Spread over cake. Then spread layer of a 20 oz. can of crushed pineapple, drained, over pudding. Then spread 1 (8 oz.) container of Cool Whip over. Then last sprinkle 1 cup crushed pecans over top. Refrigerate. (Do not over bake cake mix as it is thin in long pan. Bake about 20 minutes. Also do not over drain pineapple.)

BANANA PUDDING

1 box vanilla wafers   3 cups cold milk
1 large box of instant vanilla pudding   1 can Eagle Brand
                                            condensed milk
1 (12 oz.) container of Cool Whip   5 or 6 bananas

Line a large bowl with vanilla wafers (2 deep on bottom). Combine milk and instant pudding. When it starts to thicken, add condensed milk and whisk until smooth. Fold in half of the Cool Whip. Into the bowl lined with vanilla wafers pour half of pudding mixture, 1 layer of sliced bananas, 1 layer of vanilla wafers, the rest of the pudding, then 1 layer of bananas. Top with rest of the Cool Whip being careful to seal the edges. Refrigerate. (This is the best recipe for banana pudding, simply luscious!)

BANANA ICE CREAM

1 quart milk   2 cups sugar
1 tablespoon flour   4 whole eggs
1 tablespoon vanilla   3 or 4 bananas

Put milk, sugar, flour and eggs into scalded milk (in top of double boiler). Let this cook until it coats a spoon, stirring often. Take off and cool. Add vanilla. Mash bananas in blender or mixer. Add a little lemon juice. Add bananas to custard, put in freezer can (electric or hand turn). Finish filling freezer can (gallon size) with half and half (light cream) or whipping cream. Freeze until hard.

AUNT IDA'S APPLE CRISP

1 (20 oz.) can apple pie filling
1 cup brown sugar
1 teaspoon cinnamon
6 tablespoons butter, melted

1/4 cup flour
1/4 teaspoon salt
1/4 teaspoon nutmeg
1 cup old fashioned oats

Pour apple pie filling in a shallow 1 quart baking dish. In bowl combine flour, oats, sugar, salt and spices. Add butter and mix well. Spread topping evenly over pie filling. Bake at 375° for 30 minutes.

LEMON ICE CREAM

1/4 cup lemon juice
1/2 cup white Karo
2 cups cream, whipped

1/2 cup sugar
2 whole eggs

Beat eggs, add lemon juice, sugar and Karo. Add whipped cream. Beat well in mixer. Put in refrigerator trays. When it freezes around the edges, stir well. Apricots added to this is delicious. (Easy way to make ice cream.)

BISHOP'S PIE DESSERT

1/2 cup butter or margarine
1/4 cup brown sugar (packed)
1 1/2 cups powdered sugar
1 (8 oz.) pkg. cream cheese

1 cup plain flour
1/2 cup nuts, chopped fine
1/2 pint whipping cream

Mix flour, butter, brown sugar and nuts together. Mix with hands and pat out in a 9 x 13 inch pan. Bake at 300° until light brown (20 to 25 min..). Let cool. Mix cream cheese, whipped cream and powdered sugar together and spread on top of crust. Refrigerate overnight. Top with cherries, strawberries, peaches or any fruit you desire when ready to serve. Serves 12 to 15. (This unusual dessert makes a hit at a dinner party.)

PISTACHIO WONDER

70 crushed Ritz crackers
2 sticks margarine, melted
2 small pkgs. instant pistachio pudding
1 1/2 cups milk
1 quart vanilla ice cream
1 large carton Cool Whip
3 Heath bars, crushed

Mix together crackers and margarine, press into a 9 x 13 inch pyrex dish. Bake 10 minutes at 350°. Cool to room temperature. Mix pudding with milk and then mix with softened ice cream. Pour into cooled cracker crust and freeze. Approximately 30 minutes before serving top with Cool Whip and garnish with crushed Heath bars. Place in refrigerator for 1 hour before cutting. Garnish with Maraschino cherries. (Very rich dessert.)

SNOWBALL CAKE (DESSERT)

2 envelopes Knox gelatin   1 cup sugar
1 cup water

Mix and stir over low heat until gelatin is dissolved.

Add:
   1 small can (8 1/4 oz.) crushed pineapple
   and juice of 1 lemon

Chill in refrigerator until slightly thickened. Prepare 2 envelopes of Dream Whip according to directions on package (or can use Cool Whip). Add to gelatin mixture.

Crumble:
   1 large angel food cake (remove brown crust) Add gelatin mixture and mix well.

Put into large pan or pyrex (9 x 13 inch)

Topping:
Prepare 2 envelopes Dream Whip according to directions on package (or Cool Whip).
Add:
   1 cup powdered sugar (do not use powdered sugar if you use Cool Whip).

Sprinkle with fresh or frozen coconut and chill. Cut in squares to serve. Top with a cherry.

Variation: Use 1 package (3 oz.) of strawberry jello and 1 package plain gelatin for a pretty pink color, or a jello to suit the season.

(This is a favorite during holidays or anytime.)

CHOCOLATE ANGEL FOOD DESSERT

1 (6 oz.) package chocolate chips   1 teaspoon vanilla
4 tablespoons water   2 eggs, separated
1 1/2 pints whipping cream, whipped   1/4 teaspoon salt
1/2 cup chopped nuts   1 medium angel food cake

Melt chocolate with 4 tablespoons water in top of double boiler or in microwave. Beat egg yolks and add chocolate a little at a time. Add salt and vanilla. Cool. Beat egg whites stiff and fold into chocolate mixture. Fold in whipped cream and nuts. Break angel food cake into bite size pieces. Line the bottom of a 9 x 13 inch pan or pyrex with angel food pieces. Pour half of chocolate mixture over it. Cover with remaining pieces of cake and pour rest of chocolate mixture over. Chill several hours. (You can use Cool Whip instead of whipped cream.) (Yummy!)

CHOCOLATE ICE CREAM CAKE

1 3/4 cups sugar
2 eggs
2 1/2 cups sifted flour
1 1/2 teaspoons soda
1 teaspoon vanilla

2/3 cup oil
1 cup buttermilk
1/2 cup cocoa
1/2 teaspoon salt
1/2 cup boiling water

Preheat oven to 350°. Cream sugar and oil. Add eggs, one at a time, beat well. Add vanilla. Sift together flour, salt, soda. Add alternately with milk to creamed mixture. Make a paste of cocoa and boiling water. Add this and blend well. Pour into greased 9 x 13 inch pan. Bake 30 to 35 minutes or until tests done. When cool (10 min.) remove from pan on wax paper. Let cool completely. Split cake, put 1/2 gallon of vanilla ice cream (softened) between split layers. Put back together. Wrap in foil. Freeze until ready to serve. It thaws in 20 minutes. This is delicious and keeps well in freezer. Serve with Fudge Sauce.

Fudge Sauce

In heavy saucepan combine 1 (6 oz.) pkg. semi-sweet chocolate chips and 2/3 cup white corn syrup. Cook and stir over low heat until chocolate chips melt. Remove from heat, cool. Gradually stir in 1 (6 oz.) can of evaporated milk.

PEACH ICE CREAM

1 quart or more of fresh peaches (mashed)
juice of 1 1/2 lemons
2 1/2 cups sugar
1 quart whole milk
2/3 cup buttermilk (buttermilk gives it a tang)
1 pint whipping cream

Mix all ingredients together and pour into freezer can. Freeze until hard. (This is the best peach ice cream you ever tasted - the buttermilk makes it taste like sherbet.)

STRAWBERRY ANGEL FOOD DELIGHT

1 small can (8 1/4 oz.) crushed pineapple
1 pkg. strawberry jello (3 oz.)
1 (10 oz.) pkg. frozen strawberries
1/2 pint whipping cream

1 cup sugar
1/4 cup lemon juice

1 small angel food cake

Mix pineapple, sugar, lemon juice and jello and let come to a boil, stirring constantly. Cool slightly and add partially thawed strawberries. Let slightly congeal and fold in whipped cream. Break cake into pieces, and cover bottom of a 13 inch pyrex flat dish with cake. Pour mixture over cake. Refrigerate. Cut into squares. Serve with whipped cream on top of squares. Garnish with a strawberry.

LEMON DESSERT

1. *1 1/2 cups flour*   *1 1/2 sticks margarine*
   2/3 cup finely chopped nuts

Mix this with your hands and press into a 9 x 13 inch pan. Bake at 350° for 20 to 25 minutes.

2. *Beat until smooth 8 oz. cream cheese, 1 cup powdered sugar and a 9 oz. pkg. Cool Whip. Whip until fluffy and spread on cooled crust.*
3. *Combine 3 cups milk and 2 pkgs. of instant lemon pudding.*

Stir until thick and pour over cheese mixture. Refrigerate until ready to serve. Serves 12 to 15. Cut in squares and top with a twist of lemon. (Delicious dessert!)

HOT FUDGE SAUCE

2 tablespoons white Karo syrup   *1 cup sugar*
1/2 cup half and half (light cream)   *1/8 teaspoon salt*
1 square unsweetened chocolate   *1 tablespoon butter*
(or 2 tablespoons cocoa)   *1 teaspoon vanilla*

Melt butter and chocolate. If you use cocoa mix it with sugar, salt, Karo, and half and half, stirring constantly. Bring to a boil, let boil for 1 minute. Add butter. Take off heat and let cool a few minutes. Then add vanilla. Serve warm over ice cream. Can reheat in microwave.

SIX THREES ICE CREAM

3 cups milk   *3 cups light cream*
3 cups sugar   *juice of 3 lemons*
juice of 3 oranges   *3 bananas, mashed*

Combine milk, cream, and sugar, stir until sugar is dissolved. Freeze in ice cream freezer until mushy. Open freezer can and add fruit juices and bananas. Continue freezing until crank turns hard. Remove dasher, pack in ice for 4 hours. Makes 3 quarts. (This is the most refreshing, delicious ice cream! A very old recipe.)

OLD FASHIONED BOILED CUSTARD

1/2 gallon whole milk   *Op, a pinch of salt*
1 1/4 cups sugar   *12/2012*
6 egg yolks
Vanilla - flavor to taste

Put milk in top of double boiler and heat until hot. Beat egg yolks with sugar. Add some of the hot milk to the egg and sugar mixture. Then add the rest of the hot milk and stir well. Put back in top of double boiler. If it won't hold it all, cook part of it until the first mixture coats a spoon & is slightly thickened, then add the rest and cook. Let water simmer (not boil) in bottom of double boiler. Stir frequently. Flavor with 1 tablespoon of vanilla and let cool. Refridgerate.

Ramsey-Pomarede

PIES AND PASTRIES

GRAHAM CRACKER CRUST

Combine 1 1/4 cups fine graham cracker crumbs, 1/4 cup sugar and 6 tablespoons melted margarine. Mix well. Press firmly into 9-inch pie plate. Bake at 375° for 6 to 8 minutes or until edges are browned. Cool. For unbaked crust, chill 45 minutes.

VANILLA WAFER CRUST

Mix together 1 1/2 cups fine vanilla wafer crumbs and 6 tablespoons melted margarine. Press firmly into 9-inch pie plate. Chill.

CHOCOLATE WAFER CRUST

Mix together 1 1/2 cups fine chocolate wafer crumbs and 6 tablespoons melted margarine. Press firmly into 9-inch pie plate. Chill.

COCONUT CRUST

Combine 1 (3 1/2 oz.) can (1 1/3 cups) flaked coconut and 2 tablespoons melted margarine. Press into 9-inch pie plate. Bake at 325° for 15 minutes or until light brown.

Freeze pies before baking (no slits in top crust). Wrap in moisture-proof material, seal, label. Bake frozen pies without thawing. Cut slits in top crust after 5 minutes of baking. Return to oven.

NEVER FAIL PIE CRUST

3 cups plain flour	*2 teaspoon salt*
1 1/4 cups shortening	*1 tablespoon sugar*
1 tablespoon vinegar	*1/2 cup water*
1 egg	

Mix the flour, shortening, sugar and salt with a pastry blender or two knives. Beat the egg, add the water and vinegar and mix well. Combine the two mixtures, a little at a time, until all dry ingredients are moist. Mold together with your hands. Chill before rolling out or keep in refrigerator up to a week. Or you can freeze it and use whatever amount you like after returning it to room temperature. Makes 2 double crust 9-inch pies and 1 (9-inch) shell.

GRATED APPLE PIE

2 1/2 cups peeled grated apples	*1 1/2 cups sugar*
1 stick melted butter	*1/2 teaspoon nutmeg*
1 slightly beaten egg	

Mix all together and put in an unbaked 9- or 10-inch pie shell. Bake at 325° for 45 minutes or until brown. (A really delicious, different apple pie.)

VANILLA CREAM PIE

In saucepan combine 3/4 cup sugar, 1/3 cup flour or 3 tablespoons cornstarch and 1/4 teaspoon salt. Gradually add 2 cups milk, mixing well. Cook and stir over medium heat until mixture thickens and boils. Cook 2 minutes longer. Remove from heat. Stir small amount of hot mixture into 3 slightly beaten egg yolks, return to hot mixture, cook 2 minutes, stirring constantly. Remove from heat. Add 2 tablespoons butter and 1 teaspoon vanilla. Pour into baked 9-inch pastry shell. Spread 1 recipe meringue (3 egg whites) on top of pie and bake at 325° for 12 to 15 minutes. Cool.

For Chocolate Cream Pie, add 3 tablespoons cocoa or chop two 1 oz. squares unsweetened chocolate and add with milk. Increase sugar to 1 cup.

For Banana Cream Pie, slice 3 bananas into cooled pie shell, top with vanilla cream filling.

For Butterscotch Cream Pie, substitute brown sugar for granulated sugar. Increase butter to 3 tablespoons.

For Coconut Cream Pie, add 1 cup flaked or frozen coconut to vanilla cream pie filling. Top with meringue, sprinkle with 1/3 cup coconut. Bake as directed.

FRENCH COCONUT PIE

4 eggs	1 stick butter
1 1/2 cups sugar	1/4 teaspoon salt
1/2 teaspoon coconut flavoring	1 teaspoon vanilla
1 tablespoon vinegar	1 cup coconut

Beat eggs, add melted butter. Stir in remaining ingredients. Pour into unbaked pie shell. Bake at 400° for 10 minutes, reduce heat to 325° and bake for 35 minutes or until set.

PECAN PIE

3 eggs, beaten	1/2 cup white Karo
1 cup sugar	1/4 teaspoon salt
1 teaspoon white vinegar	1 cup chopped pecans
1/2 stick butter or margarine, melted	1 teaspoon vanilla

Mix all ingredients and pour into unbaked 9-inch pie shell. Bake at 375° for 35 minutes or until set. (Of all the pecan pie recipes I've tried, this is the best—not so dead sweet and syrupy.)

CREOLE PECAN PIE

1 (9 inch) unbaked pie shell
4 tablespoons butter, softened
1/2 cup cane syrup (no substitute)
1/2 cup light corn syrup
1 cup chopped pecans
2 teaspoons grated orange rind
1 cup whipping cream, whipped

1/2 cup sugar
3 eggs
1/4 teaspoon salt
1 teaspoon vanilla
1/2 cup pecan halves

In a bowl, cream butter and sugar. Add eggs, one at a time, beating until light and fluffy. Add syrups, salt, vanilla, chopped pecans and orange rind, blend well. Pour into pie shell. Arrange pecan halves over top of pie. Bake at 350° for 45 minutes or until firm when gently shaken. Remove and cool. Serve with whipped cream. (The luscious Louisiana version of pecan pie.)

SWEET POTATO PECAN PIE

Line a 9-inch pie plate with pastry.

Filling:
1 1/2 cups mashed sweet potatoes
1/2 cup brown sugar, packed
1 1/2 cups scalded milk
2 well-beaten eggs

1 teaspoon ginger
1 teaspoon cinnamon
1/4 teaspoon salt

Mix well and pour into unbaked pie shell. Bake at 350° for 20 minutes, then sprinkle on topping:

1/2 cup packed brown sugar
1/4 cup butter or margarine
3/4 cup finely chopped pecans

Mix these ingredients together and sprinkle over top of pie. Continue baking until custard is set, about 45 minutes in all. Serve with whipped cream. (This is the best sweet potato pie you ever tasted!)

BLACKBERRY COBBLER

6 cups blackberries
2 tablespoons cornstarch
1 tablespoon cinnamon (optional

1/2 cup sugar
2 tablespoons lemon juice

Topping:
1/2 cup butter or margarine, softened
4 teaspoons baking powder
1/2 teaspoon salt

1 cup sugar
2 cups flour
1 cup milk

Toss berries with filling ingredients except butter. Place in a wide casserole (11 x 7-inch glass dish). Dot with butter. To mix pastry, beat butter, add sugar and mix well. Add remaining ingredients until just combined. Drop pastry dough on top of blackberries. Sprinkle with sugar if desired. Bake at 350° for 40 minutes. Pastry should be golden brown. Serves 8. Serve with vanilla ice cream.

GRASSHOPPER PIE

14 hydrox cookies (Oreo) (without icing) or chocolate ice box cookies
1/4 cup melted butter or margarine (cooled)

Crush cookies and mix thoroughly with melted butter. Press into 9-inch pie pan and cook at 400° for 5 to 10 minutes.

Filling:
26 large marshmallows
1/2 cup milk
1/2 pint whipping cream, whipped
4 tablespoons creme de menthe
4 tablespoons creme de cacao

Melt marshmallows in milk in top of double boiler. Let cool. Fold in rest of ingredients. Pour into baked pie shell and refrigerate. (This can be frozen.)

STRAWBERRY PIE

1 cup sugar   *6 teaspoons cornstarch*
1 cup water   *red food color*

Cook these ingredients until clear and thick. Add 4 tablespoons of strawberry jello. Stir well. Cool. Put sliced fresh strawberries in bottom of baked 9-inch pastry shell. Pour cooled mixture over berries. Refrigerate. Serve with whipping cream on top. (Luscious!)

BLUSH APPLE PIE

5 large apples, sliced thin   *1 teaspoon lemon juice*
1 small can (8 oz.) crushed pineapple, *1 1/4 cups sugar*
*   drained*   *2 tablespoons butter*
3 tablespoons plain flour   *1/4 teaspoon salt*
1/4 cup cinnamon drops

Sift sugar, flour and salt together. In large bowl combine apples, pineapple, cinnamon drops, lemon juice. Add dry ingredients over apple mixture. Stir several times while making pastry. Pour into 9-inch pie pan lined with pastry. Place pastry over top, dot with butter and cut slits in top pastry. Bake at 350° until done and brown.

WILLIAMSBURG APPLE PIE

2 cups unsifted flour
2/3 cup margarine
1/2 cup apricot preserves
1 teaspoon grated lemon peel
4 cups diced, peeled cooking apples
1/4 teaspoon cinnamon
2 tablespoons butter or margarine

1 teaspoon salt
7 tablespoons ice water
1 tablespoon lemon juice
1/2 cup sugar
3 tablespoons flour
1/4 teaspoon nutmeg

Measure 2 cups flour and salt in bowl. Cut in 2/3 cup margarine with pastry blender or knives until mixture resembles coarse meal. Gradually sprinkle in ice water, stirring well after each addition. Gather into a ball. On lightly floured board roll out 1/2 of the dough to fit a 10-inch deep pie plate. Combine preserves, lemon peel and juice. Mix in apples. Combine sugar, flour, and spices and add to apple mixture. Dot with 2 tablespoons butter. Roll out remaining pastry for top crust. Make slits to allow steam to escape during baking. Place over filling, seal and finish edges. If glaze is desired, brush pastry with beaten egg. Bake at 400° for 10 minutes, reduce heat to 350° and bake until done. (This is the most unusual, best apple pie you ever tasted!)

JAPANESE FRUIT PIE

1/2 stick margarine
2 eggs
1/2 cup raisins
1/2 cup chopped pecans

1/2 cup coconut
1 cup sugar
1 tablespoon vinegar

Melt margarine, cool, add rest of ingredients. Put in unbaked 8-inch pie shell. Bake at 325° for 40 minutes. (This pie is best served warm. Freezes well. Mm good!)

SOUR CREAM APPLE PIE

2 cups diced apples
1 teaspoon vanilla

1 cup sour cream
1 egg

Mix these ingredients together.

3/4 cup sugar
1/2 teaspoon salt

2 tablespoons plain flour
1/4 teaspoon nutmeg

Mix together and mix with apple mixture. Pour into unbaked pie shell and bake 30 minutes at 350°.

Topping:
1/3 cup sugar
1/2 cup flour

1 teaspoon cinnamon
1/4 cup butter (melted)

Take pie out of oven and sprinkle mixture over top. Bake at 400° until golden brown.

SKILLET CHOCOLATE PIE

3 egg yolks
3 tablespoons plain flour
1 1/2 cups milk
1 teaspoon vanilla

1 cup sugar
3 tablespoons cocoa
2 tablespoons butter

Mix milk and egg yolks in heavy iron skillet. Add flour, cocoa, and sugar which have been sifted together. Cook over low heat till thick. Add butter and vanilla. Put in baked 9-inch pie shell. Make meringue of 3 egg whites, 6 tablespoons sugar and spread on top of filling. Bake at 325° until brown. (An easy custard chocolate pie.) To prevent shrinking of meringue, carefully seal meringue to edge of pastry shell.

CHOCOLATE CHESS PIE

1/2 stick butter
3 tablespoons cocoa
1/2 cup evaporated milk

1 1/2 cups sugar
2 whole eggs
1 teaspoon vanilla

Melt butter in heavy saucepan. Add sugar and cocoa. Stir well. Add eggs. Stir mixture, do not beat. Add milk and vanilla. Pour into 8- or 9-inch unbaked pie shell. Bake at 400° for 10 minutes, reduce heat to 350° and bake for 20 to 25 minutes. (Good served with vanilla ice cream.)

CHOCOLATE MERINGUE PIE

1 1/2 cups sugar
2 tablespoons all-purpose flour
1 teaspoon vanilla extract
2 tablespoons melted butter or margarine
1 unbaked 8- or 9-inch pastry shell
1/4 teaspoon cream of tartar

3 eggs, separated
3/4 cup milk
6 tablespoons sugar
3 tablespoons cocoa

Combine 1 1/2 cups sugar, flour, and cocoa; set aside. Combine egg yolks and milk, beating well; add to dry mixture. Add butter and vanilla, mixing well. Pour into pastry shell. Bake at 400° for 10 minutes; reduce heat to 325° and bake for 30 minutes or until set. Cool.

Beat egg whites until soft peaks form. Gradually add 6 tablespoons sugar and cream of tartar. Continue beating until stiff peaks form and sugar is dissolved. Spread meringue over filling, sealing edges well. Bake at 325° for 8 to 10 minutes or until lightly browned.

(This is a very old recipe. This was our favorite pie when I was a child and is my children's favorite too.)

CARAMEL PIE

Put a can of Eagle Brand sweetened condensed milk in deep saucepan (do not open can). Fill saucepan with water—be sure can is covered with water all the time. Bring water to a boil, then simmer for 2 1/2 hours. Take out of water and let cool, then open can. Do not open can until it cools. Spoon into baked plain pie shell or a graham cracker crust. Let cool completely then cover with whipped cream or Cool Whip. Refrigerate. (Very rich and delicious.)

FRIED PIES

Cook a package of dried fruit (apricots, apples or peaches) in water to cover until tender. Drain and strain through ricer or sieve. Sweeten and flavor to taste. Make pastry not as rich as for pies. Roll out and cut in small circles. Put a dab of fruit on each circle and a dot of butter. Fold, mash edges with a fork. Fry in hot fat. Drain on paper towels. (An old favorite.)

COUNTRY COUSIN PIE

3 egg whites	1 cup sugar
1 teaspoon vanilla	18 soda crackers, crushed
1/2 cup pecans, chopped fine	1 package Dream Whip or
6 teaspoons pineapple preserves	Cool Whip topping

Beat egg whites until foamy. Add 1 cup sugar gradually. Beat very stiff. Add vanilla. fold in crushed crackers and nuts. Bake in lightly greased 9-inch pie plate or a 10 x 6-inch pan at 325° for 25 to 30 minutes. Let cool. Prepare Dream Whip according to directions and fold in pineapple preserves. Spread over baked meringue crust. Sprinkle with coconut (I prefer frozen) and chill. (This is sometimes known as Soda Cracker Pie.) You can vary the fillings. I like this lemon filling:

4 egg yolks	1 tablespoon lemon rind
1/2 cup sugar	1/8 teaspoon salt
3 tablespoons lemon juice	1 cup cream, whipped

Beat egg yolks slightly, stir in sugar, lemon juice, rind and salt. Cook over boiling water until thick. Cool. Fold in whipped cream. Spoon into shell and chill in refrigerator until ready to serve.

LEMON MERINGUE PIE

1 1/2 cups sugar
3 tablespoons flour
1 1/2 cups hot water
3 slightly beaten egg yolks
1/2 teaspoon grated lemon peel
1 baked 9-inch pastry shell

3 tablespoons cornstarch
dash of salt
2 tablespoons butter
1/3 cup lemon juice
1 recipe meringue (3 egg
   whites)

In saucepan, mix sugar, cornstarch, flour, and salt. Gradually add hot water, stirring constantly. Cook and stir over high heat till mixture comes to boiling. Reduce heat, cook and stir 2 minutes. Stir small amount of hot mixture into egg yolks, then return to hot mixture. Bring to boiling and cook 2 minutes, stirring constantly. Add butter and lemon peel. Slowly add lemon juice, mixing well. Pour into pastry shell. Spread meringue over filling. Bake at 300° to 325° till brown. Cool before serving. (This is a perfect lemon pie if you follow directions exactly.)

MERINGUE

3 egg whites
1/2 teaspoon salt
1/4 teaspoon cream of tartar

1 tablespoon water
6 tablespoons sugar

Beat egg whites, water, salt, cream of tartar until foamy. Gradually add sugar and beat until very stiff. Pile on pie and bake at 300° to 325° for 15 or 20 minutes. Let cool slowly.

PUMPKIN ORANGE CRUNCH PIE

1 cup brown sugar (packed)
1 1/2 teaspoon pumpkin pie spice
1 (1 lb.) can (2 cups) pumpkin
1 (14 1/2 oz.) can (1 2/3 cups) evaporated milk
1 unbaked 9-inch pastry shell (or 10-inch)

1 tablespoon cornstarch
1/4 teaspoon salt
2 slightly beaten eggs

Topping:
   1 tablespoon brown sugar
   1 tablespoon butter or margarine
   1 tablespoon all-purpose flour
   1/2 cup finely chopped pecans or walnuts
   2 teaspoons grated orange peel

Combine 1 cup brown sugar, cornstarch, pie spice, salt and pumpkin. Stir in milk and eggs. Pour into pastry shell. (Crimp edges high, filling is generous.) Bake at 375° for 40 minutes. Meanwhile, combine topping ingredients. Spoon over pie, return to oven and bake 5 to 10 minutes more or until knife comes out clean. Cool.

(A different, delicious pumpkin pie.)

COCONUT MACAROON PIE

3 eggs, separated
1 1/2 cups sugar
2 tablespoons butter
1/4 teaspoon almond extract
1 1/2 cups shredded coconut, cut
1 unbaked 9-inch pastry shell

1/4 teaspoon salt
1/4 cup milk
1 teaspoon lemon juice
1 teaspoon vanilla

Beat egg yolks and salt until thick and lemon colored. Add sugar 1/2 cup at a time, beating well after each addition. Add milk, butter, lemon juice, almond extract and vanilla. Blend well. Beat egg whites until stiff. Fold coconut and beaten whites into the yolk mixture. Turn into unbaked pie shell. Bake at 375° for 45 to 50 minutes or until knife inserted comes out clean. (A crunchy macaroon-like mixture rises to the top, leaving a delicate custard layer below; very delicious.)

BROWN SUGAR CHESS PIE

2 whole eggs
1/2 cup brown sugar
1/4 cup melted butter
1/2 teaspoon vinegar
1 teaspoon flour

1 cup white sugar
1/4 cup milk
1/2 teaspoon vanilla
1 teaspoon corn meal

Mix all ingredients together. Pour into 8- or 9-inch unbaked pie shell. Bake at 350° for 25 to 30 minutes. (Pecans added to this make a delicious pecan pie.)

EASY COCONUT PIE

1 cup coconut (fresh or canned)
1/2 cup buttermilk
1 teaspoon vanilla
dash of salt

1 cup sugar
2 eggs
1/2 stick butter, melted

Mix all ingredients together. Pour into unbaked 8- or 9-inch pie shell. Bake at 325° for 45 minutes.

PECAN TARTS

Cream Cheese Pastry
1 stick butter or margarine
1 (3 oz.) pkg. cream cheese
1 cup flour (plain)

Covering Mixture
1 egg, beaten
3/4 cup brown sugar, packed
1 tsp vanilla
1 tablespoon butter
Dash of salt

Mix Pastry ingredients with your hands. Pinch off enough dough each time to press into small tart pans or small muffin tins. Sprinkle into each tart or muffin pan some finely chopped pecans. Barely cover with Covering Mixture. Bake at 350 until set and light brown. Yield: 24 tiny tarts. (Yummy!) (Great for parties.) These are sometimes known as Tea Time Tassies.

CHESS PIE

1 1/3 cups sugar
1/2 cup butter
1 tablespoon corn meal
1 teaspoon vanilla

1/3 cup coffee cream
1 teaspoon white vinegar
3 whole eggs

Make 9-inch pastry shell. Refrigerate until filling is made. Cream butter and sugar together until light and fluffy. Add meal, cream and vinegar. Add eggs, one at a time, beating after each addition. Blend in vanilla. Pour into chilled unbaked pie shell. Bake at 350° for 45 minutes or until light brown and set. Pie will be shaky in the center but will set when it cools. Let cool 1 hour before serving. (My favorite chess pie recipe.)

LEMON CHESS PIE

4 whole eggs
2 cups sugar
grated rind of 1 lemon, if desired
1 tablespoon flour

1/4 cup milk or cream
1/4 cup lemon juice
1 tablespoon corn meal
1/3 cup melted butter

Mix all ingredients together and pour into unbaked 9- or 10-inch pie shell. Bake at 400° for 10 minutes, reduce heat to 325° and bake until set. (The lemon gives it a good flavor.)

CHERRY PIE

1 can sour cherries
1 cup sugar

1/4 teaspoon salt
3 tablespoons cornstarch

Mix this together and cook until thick in heavy saucepan. Then add 1/4 teaspoon almond extract, 1/2 teaspoon red food color, and 2 tablespoons butter and 1 tablespoon lemon juice. Pour into 10-inch unbaked pie shell. Strip top and sprinkle with a little sugar. Bake at 400° for 10 minutes, reduce heat to 350° and bake until brown.

CHERRY PIE DELUXE

1 can sour pitted cherries
7 tablespoons cornstarch
1 small can (8 oz.) crushed pineapple
1/2 teaspoon salt
4 bananas

2 cups sugar
1 teaspoon red food color
2 teaspoon vanilla
1 cup pecans, chopped

Drain juice from cherries and pineapple and add water to make 2 cups. Add sugar, cornstarch and salt and red food color. Cook in saucepan until thick. Let cool. Add cherries, pineapple, bananas, vanilla and pecans. Pour into individual tart shells (baked) or 2 large baked pie shells. Top with whipped cream or Cool Whip. (Superb!)

APPLE DUMPLINGS

Peel and core 6 medium tart apples. Cut into small pieces. Roll out pie crust thin; cut 6 rounds the size of a saucer. Into each pastry round put minced apple, 2 tablespoons sugar, 1/4 teaspoon lemon juice, 5 or 6 pecan meats, broken into small pieces, 1 teaspoon butter, dash of cinnamon and nutmeg. Pinch pastry round together at top, prick with a fork to allow steam to escape. Over top of each dumpling put dab of butter, sprinkle lightly with sugar and cinnamon. In the meantime boil the peeling of the apples in water until soft. Put 1 1/2 cups of this liquid around dumplings in pan. Add 3/4 cup sugar and 1/2 teaspoon vanilla. Cook about 30 minutes at 375°, basting occasionally with liquid. (This is a very old recipe and different from most.)

EASY PEACH COBBLER

1 large can freestone peaches (sliced) or
*   1 quart frozen peaches (do not drain)*
1 cup sugar or to taste
1/2 cup orange juice and grated orange peel
2 tablespoons flour to thicken

Put all above ingredients into large saucepan and heat until syrupy. Pour into oblong pyrex dish. Sprinkle 1 package of Jiffy Cake Mix (dry), then drizzle 1 stick butter or margarine over all. Bake at 350° until light brown. Serve warm with vanilla ice cream on top.

CHOCOLATE CHIP PIE

Melt 1 stick butter or margarine. Add 1 cup sugar. Mix together. Add 2 eggs, slightly beaten and 1 teaspoon vanilla. Stir in 1 cup chocolate chips and 1 cup chopped nuts. Pour into a 9-inch unbaked pie shell and bake at 350°-375° for 35 to 40 minutes or until set. (Good served with vanilla ice cream.)

ORANGE PIE

1 1/4 cups sugar
3 eggs
1/2 stick butter, melted
1/2 cup coconut
1/2 cup frozen orange juice concentrate, undiluted
1 teaspoon lemon extract

Beat eggs and add rest of ingredients. Pour into unbaked 9 inch pie shell. Bake at 400° for 10 minutes, reduce heat to 325° and bake for 25 minutes or until set. (Delightful tart flavor.)

BLACK BOTTOM PIE

Crust:

1 1/3 cups crushed gingersnaps   *2 tablespoons sugar*
1/3 cup soft butter or margarine
1 bar German sweet chocolate, divided

Mix gingersnaps, butter and sugar. Shave chocolate and add 1/2 to gingersnap mixture, stirring well. Press into bottom and sides of a 9-inch pie pan or plate. Bake in 350° for 6 to 8 minutes.

Filling:

1 package vanilla pudding mix   *2 cups light cream*
1 cup heavy cream, whipped   *1 1/2 cups milk*
1 package chocolate pudding mix   *1/3 cup light rum*

Blend together vanilla pudding mix, 1 1/2 cups light cream and rum. Bring to a boil, stirring constantly. Pour into pie crust, cover with wax paper, chill. Blend together chocolate pudding mix, 1/2 cup light cream, milk, and remaining half of shaved chocolate. Bring to a boil, stirring constantly. Pour over first layer. Cover with wax paper and chill. Before serving, top with whipped cream. (A delicious party pie.)

LAZY PIE

1 stick butter, melted
1 cup plain flour
1 cup sugar
1/8 teaspoon salt
1 tablespoon baking powder
2/3 cup milk
2 1/2 cups sweetened blackberries with juice or any fruit you desire

Heat oven to 350°. Melt butter in 2 quart casserole. Sift together dry ingredients. Add milk and stir together. Pour batter into casserole with butter. Do not stir. Add fruit. Do not stir. Bake for about 45 minutes, or until nicely browned. (May be served hot or cold, with ice cream or plain. This resembles a cobbler pie.)

Ramsey-Pomarede

MEATS AND ENTREES

BUTTERMILK FRIED CHICKEN

1 cup buttermilk
1 teaspoon salt
1/4 teaspoon pepper (optional)
1 (2 1/2 to 3 lb. broiler-fryer, cut up
1 cup all-purpose flour
1 1/2 cups vegetable oil or can use vegetable shortening

Combine buttermilk, salt and pepper; stir well. Place chicken in a shallow container and pour buttermilk mixture over top of chicken. Cover and let stand 20 minutes, turning once. Remove chicken. Dredge chicken in flour, coating well. Cook in hot oil 350° or shortening (iron skillet preferred) until browned, turning to brown both sides. Reduce heat to 275°, cover and cook 20 to 25 minutes. Uncover and cook an additional 5 minutes. Drain on paper towels. (The buttermilk tenderizes the chicken and gives it a good taste.)(Any time you cook chicken, always soak it in cold salt water before cooking.)

HAM AND TURKEY DIVAN

2 (10 oz.) pkgs. frozen broccoli
1 can cream of chicken soup, undiluted
1/2 cup sharp grated cheese
8 slices cooked ham
1/2 cup whipping cream, whipped
1 tablespoon butter or margarine, melted
1/2 cup mayonnaise
1 teaspoon lemon juice
8 slices cooked turkey
1/2 teaspoon curry powder
1/2 cup soft bread crumbs

Prepare broccoli and drain. Arrange broccoli in lightly greased baking dish. Top with slices of turkey and ham. Blend soup with mayonnaise, lemon juice and curry. Fold in whipped cream. Spoon over broccoli and meat. Sprinkle with grated cheese. Bake at 350° for 20 to 30 minutes. (You can use chicken instead of turkey.) (This is an elegant dish to serve at a luncheon or dinner party.

CHICKEN EUGENE

3 to 4 chicken breasts, halved, deboned and skinned
salt to taste
6 to 8 thin slices cooked ham
1/2 cup melted butter
1/2 cup sherry
1 can mushroom soup, undiluted
1 (8 oz.) carton sour cream
paprika
1 (4 oz.) can sliced mushrooms, drained

Sprinkle chicken with salt and paprika. Place ham slices in a shallow baking dish, top with chicken. Combine remaining ingredients, blending well. Pour over chicken. Bake at 350° for 1 to 1 1/2 hours or until done. (Wonderful blend of flavors. Good served with rice.)

CHEESE STUFFED MEATBALLS

1 1/2 lbs. lean ground beef
1 small garlic clove, minced
1/3 cup dry bread crumbs
1/4 lb. cheddar cheese, cut into
   approximately 30 pieces
1/4 cup butter or margarine
1 cup dry red wine

1 teaspoon salt
1 egg lightly beaten
1/3 cup milk
flour

Mix together meat, garlic, egg, bread crumbs, salt and milk. Form meatballs around cubes of cheese and roll in flour, shaking off excess. Saute meatballs in butter, turning often until well browned. Drain off fat. Add wine, cover skillet and simmer about 10 minutes. (Makes about 30 one inch balls (Good to serve at a party.)

NEW ORLEANS SHRIMP SAUCE

2 cloves garlic, chopped fine
1/2 cup chili sauce or ketchup
1 tablespoon Worcestershire sauce
1 teaspoon prepared mustard
juice of 1 lemon

1/2 cup oil
1 cup mayonnaise
dash of paprika
dash of tabasco
1 medium onion, grated

Mix all ingredients well and place in refrigerator for a few hours. (Delicious on shrimp.)

DEVILED SWISS STEAK

1/4 cup flour
1 1/2 teaspoon dry mustard
1 (3 lb.) round steak, cut 1 1/2
   inches thick
1 tablespoon Worcestershire sauce
1 (3 oz.) can broiled mushroom crowns, drained

1 teaspoon salt
1 teaspoon pepper
1/4 cup oil
1/2 cup water

Combine flour, salt, pepper, and dry mustard. Sprinkle mixture over round steak and pound into meat. In heavy skillet, brown steak slowly on both sides in hot oil. Combine water and Worcestershire sauce, add to browned meat in skillet. Cover tightly and cook over very low heat for 1 3/4 to 2 hours or until tender. Remove steak to serving platter. Serve with mushrooms which have been heated in a small amount of butter or margarine. Skim excess fat from meat juices and serve with steak. Can thicken for gravy. (6 to 8 servings)

SALMON CROQUETTES

1 can salmon (pour off juice) and bone well
Season to taste with red pepper and a little salt
1 tablespoon tomato sauce
1 tablespoon melted butter
1 egg, slightly beaten
cracker crumbs

Mix well and shape into croquettes. Roll in cracker crumbs. Fry in hot fat.

CAJUN BAKED FISH

1/3 cup mayonnaise
1/2 teaspoon onion powder
1/4 teaspoon garlic powder
1/2 cup crushed sesame crackers

1/2 teaspoon cumin
1/4 teaspoon red pepper
1 lb. fish fillets

Combine mayonnaise and seasonings. Brush fish with mixture. Coat with cracker crumbs. Bake at 350° for 30 minutes or until fish flakes.

BROILED FISH

Pat fish dry with paper towel. Brush broiler rack with oil. Brush fish with basting sauce and broil about four inches from heat. check for doneness by piercing fish with fork. The fish should be flaky but moist.

Basting sauce:
2 tablespoons oil
2 tablespoons lemon juice
1/4 teaspoon paprika
1/2 teaspoon seasoned salt
1/4 teaspoon thyme

Mix all ingredients together and brush over fish while broiling, a couple of times. (Good low calorie way to serve fish.)

BIRDS (QUAIL OR DOVES)

1 box fresh mushrooms
8 birds (or a few more)
1 teaspoon parsley
2 tablespoons white wine for each bird
Enough butter or margarine to brown birds

1 clove garlic
1 teaspoon thyme
1 medium onion, chopped
1/2 cup chicken broth

Brown birds after they have been salted and peppered. Take birds out. Add onions, garlic and mushrooms. Brown slowly. Add broth, seasoning and wine. Put birds back in and simmer for 1 hour or until birds are tender. Serve with rice. (A really tasty recipe for birds.)

BEEF WITH WINE

1 chuck or a flat roast (5 or 6 lbs.)
1 pkg. dry onion soup mix
1 cup dry red wine
1 lb. mushrooms (optional)

Brown meat in small amount of fat in heavy roaster. Add dry soup and wine. Cover and simmer slowly until tender for 3 or 4 hours. Cool and skim off fat. Trim meat of fat, de-bone and cut in serving pieces. Saute whole mushrooms. Put over meat. Make gravy from liquid meat was cooked in by making a paste of flour and water and add to liquid that is hot but not boiling. Stir until smooth. (This is a delicious way to cook an inexpensive cut of meat, do not season meat with salt and pepper as onion soup mix is just the right seasoning.)

ROAST CHICKEN

1. Season chicken inside and out with salt, pepper and lemon juice.
2. Inside, put a large lump of butter and a piece of lemon peel.
3. Put a buttered, grease proof paper around bird. Oven temperature 350°.
4. After 15 minutes of cooking, turn bird over and turn oven down to 325°. If the bird is big (weight of 4-5 lbs.) you can wait 5 more minutes before turning oven down.
5. After 15 or 20 minutes take paper away.
6. Baste with more butter.
7. Cook until done, depending on weight. (Use drippings for gravy.)

(This recipe is not for a hen, a roasting chicken is larger than a fryer, but not as large as a hen.)(My daughter, Betty, cooked this when I visited her in Boston.) (I think it is the best roast chicken I've ever tasted. Be sure to use real butter for best taste.)

PARTY CHICKEN

8 halves of chicken breast (boned and skinned)
8 slices bacon
1 cup sour cream
3 oz. jar of sliced dried beef
1 can cream of mushroom soup
1 teaspoon Worcestershire sauce
1/2 teaspoon seasoned salt
1 teaspoon parsley flakes
1 teaspoon Kikkoman soy sauce
10 drops tabasco sauce

Pour boiling water over dried, shredded beef. Let stand for 3 minutes and drain. Arrange on bottom of 12 x 8 x 2 inch baking dish or broiler pan. Wrap each chicken breast with a slice of bacon and fasten with a toothpick. Place on top of beef. Combine soup, sour cream and seasonings. Spoon over chicken. Bake uncovered at 300° for 1 1/2 to 2 hours. Baste occasionally. Serves 8. (This is so flavorful and is ideal for a luncheon or dinner party.)

TURKEY IN A SACK

1 teaspoon pepper
3 teaspoons paprika
1 cup peanut oil (be sure to use peanut oil)
1 turkey (14 to 16 lbs.)

2 teaspoons salt
4 teaspoons hot water

Combine pepper, salt, paprika and hot water. Let stand at least 10 minutes. Add peanut oil and mix thoroughly. Wash and dry turkey. Rub some of the peanut oil mixture into the inside of the turkey and outside of turkey. Truss as desired. Pour remaining oil and additional oil into large paper sack (type used in grocery store - large heavy duty, and be sure it has not been recycled). Rub oil into inside of sack until every pore in every inch of sack is sealed with the oil mixture. Place turkey in sack, breast side up. Fold over end of the sack and tie securely. Bake in a 325° oven approximately 10 minutes per pound. Since the sack is airtight, the turkey is cooked by live steam, so when you open the sack, be careful! You will not have to baste since the oil sealed sack is self-basting. The turkey comes out tender and golden brown.

CHICKEN AND DRESSING

Salt a hen inside and out (can put a piece of celery in cavity), put in roaster with about 2 cups water. cover roaster and cook on top of stove or in a 350° oven until tender. Let set and skim off some of the fat before making gravy or dressing.

Corn Bread Dressing

3 cups crumbled cornbread (egg bread)
2 cups crumbled biscuits
1 cup crumbled lightbread
1 small onion, chopped fine
1 1/2 to 2 cups chopped celery
2 cups broth from chicken
1 can mushroom soup, undiluted
hot water added to mixture to make dressing the right consistency
    (not too stiff)
black pepper and red pepper to taste
sage to taste, if desired (fresh sage preferred)

Mix all ingredients together in large bowl. I do not sauté onions and celery but you can if you prefer. Put dressing in large pan and bake at 350° for 30 to 40 minutes until done and slightly brown. Do not let cook until dry. Serve around chicken or turkey.

EASY CHICKEN POT PIE

1 chicken, cooked and cut in bite size pieces
1 can cream of chicken soup, mixed with
1 can chicken broth or broth from chicken
1 can Veg-All, drained
1 onion, chopped
1/2 cup flour
1 cup cooked rice
1/2 cup milk
1 stick butter or margarine, melted

Mix chicken, Veg-All, chicken soup, chicken broth, onion and rice. Put in large buttered casserole. Mix flour, milk and melted butter. Pour over pie. Bake at 350° for 40 or 45 minutes. (Easy and good.)

CHICKEN ENCHILADAS

1/2 cup onion, chopped
2 tablespoons butter or margarine
2 cups cooked chicken, chopped
1 can enchilada sauce
12 tortillas

1 cup heavy cream
salt to taste
1 cup chicken broth
1 cup sour cream
2 cups grated cheese

Sauté onions in butter, combine with chicken. Mix cream, broth, enchilada sauce, sour cream and salt, heat. Dip tortillas in sauce until pliable. Place chicken mixture on tortillas and roll up. Place seam side down in pan, cover with sauce. Sprinkle with cheese. Bake in 350° oven until hot and cheese melts. Serves 6. (Good)

CHICKEN SQUARES WITH MUSHROOM SAUCE

1 (5 lb.) stewed chicken (about 4 cups, cut up)
  reserve 3 cups chicken broth
1 cup chopped celery
2 cups coarse soft bread crumbs
1/4 cup chopped pimento
4 eggs, beaten well

1 cup cooked rice
1 teaspoon salt
dash of cayenne

Add eggs to chicken broth and blend lightly then add other ingredients and mix lightly. Place in greased baking dish and bake 1 hour at 350° or until set. Remove from oven and let set at least 10 minutes before cutting into squares. Serve with mushroom sauce — 1 can cream of mushroom soup heated to simmer, add 1/2 cup cream, white pepper to taste and 1 tablespoon sherry. Serve hot over chicken squares. Serves 12-15. (Delicious for a ladies' luncheon.)

CHICKEN DELICIOUS

8 chicken breasts
3/4 cup bread crumbs (pre-packaged)
1/3 cup finely chopped parsley
1 clove garlic, chopped fine

2 teaspoons salt
1 teaspoon pepper
1/2 cup Parmesan cheese
1 stick butter, melted

Mix garlic and melted butter. Dip the chicken breasts in the butter and garlic mixture, then in the dry mixture. Place in 8 x 10 inch baking dish or broiler pan skin side up and bake about 1 1/2 hours at 325°. Do not turn. Do not cook until dry. Cook until brown on the outside and juicy inside. (You can use more bread crumbs and cheese, depending on size of the chicken breasts.)(You can use garlic salt instead of garlic if you prefer, but be sure to omit salt if you do.) (This is a delicious luncheon dish.)

BACON GOURMET

1 teaspoon prepared mustard
2 teaspoons Worcestershire sauce
bread crumbs

1 egg yolk
5 thin slices bacon

Beat mustard and Worcestershire sauce in egg yolk, dip bacon in this, roll in bread crumbs to cover, broil slowly on rack in oven 20 minutes at 250° until brown. (Different and good.)

BARBECUE SAUCE

1/2 cup ketchup
4 tablespoons water
1 teaspoon salt
1 teaspoon paprika
3 tablespoons brown sugar
1 tablespoon chili powder (optional)
2 tablespoons Worcestershire sauce

4 tablespoons vinegar
1 tablespoon lemon juice
1 teaspoon dry mustard
1/2 teaspoon black pepper
3 or 4 drops Tabasco

Mix all ingredients together and use this sauce for barbecued chicken, ribs or pork.

PIZZA PORK

4 (1/2 inch thick) pork tenderloin steaks
1 (8 oz.) can tomato sauce
1 (8 oz.) can pizza sauce
1 small onion, chopped
1 tablespoon parsley flakes (dried)
dash of Worcestershire sauce
1/4 cup dry red wine or sherry
1 (8 oz.) can sliced mushrooms

garlic powder
pepper
1 bay leaf
1 teaspoon oregano
Parmesan cheese

Trim excess fat from steaks and place in a greased 9 inch square pan. Sprinkle generously with garlic powder and pepper. Combine sauces, seasoning and onion. Pour over steaks or chops and sprinkle with Parmesan cheese. Cover and bake at 275° for 1 1/2 hours. Add wine and mushrooms and bake another 30 minutes. Serve with rice, noodles or spaghetti. (Very tasty!)

BARBECUED CHICKEN HALVES

Cook over slow burning charcoals for 1 hour to 1 1/2 hours, basting with barbecue sauce and turning every 15 minutes until done.

Barbecue sauce - Simmer until blended the following ingredients:

1 lb. butter or margarine
1 cup vinegar
2 teaspoon red pepper
2 teaspoons salt
3 buds of garlic, chopped

(This is a delicious, clear barbecue sauce.)

CREAMED CHICKEN

1/3 cup butter
1/2 cup chopped onion
1/2 cup chopped celery
2 cups chicken broth
1/4 teaspoon Worcestershire sauce
2 cups cooked, chopped chicken

1/3 cup flour
1/4 teaspoon thyme
3/4 cup milk
salt to taste
dash of tabasco sauce

Melt butter or margarine over low heat, add onion and celery, cook until light brown. Add flour and seasoning. Blend until smooth. Gradually stir in milk and broth, cook until thick. Add chicken. Allow to cook for 5 to 10 minutes, stirring as little as possible. Serve with hot cornbread squares or a cornbread ring. (The old Southern favorite, chicken on egg bread.)

MARINADE FOR MEATS

3/4 cup soy sauce (Kikkoman)
1/2 cup lemon juice
1/4 cup Worcestershire sauce
1 tablespoon prepared mustard

1/4 cup oil
1 teaspoon black pepper
3 cloves garlic, minced

Mix all ingredients together. Marinate steaks, roast or any meat in this. Refrigerate for several hours. (Makes meats tender and delicious.)

BROILED DEVILED HAMBURGERS

1 lb. ground beef
dash of Worcestershire sauce
2 teaspoons prepared mustard
2 teaspoons minced onion
buns

4 tablespoons ketchup
1/2 teaspoon salt
dash of pepper
2 teaspoons horseradish

Combine meat and seasonings. Split buns, spread with meat mixture, broil 6 minutes, having meat 3 inches from unit. Serve hot. Serves 4 or 5. (This is a different way to serve hamburgers.)

MILLION DOLLAR STEW

2 lbs. round or sirloin steak, cut up in small pieces. Brown it in butter. Add onion slices and brown. Add salt & pepper to taste. Add 1 tablespoon flour, a chopped garlic button, bay leaf, 1 can consomme', 1/2 cup red wine and 1 cup water. Put all in large roaster. Add 1 can mushrooms, 1 bunch carrots, sliced or cut up. Cook in slow oven (300°) for 1 hour or longer. Serve on rice or mashed potatoes. (This stew is tasty enough to serve to company.)

VEAL PARMESAN

2 tablespoons butter
2/3 cup evaporated milk
1/2 cup plus 2 tablespoons
 Parmesan cheese
1 (8 oz.) can tomato sauce

4 slices veal
1/4 cup flour
1/2 teaspoon salt
dash of pepper

Preheat oven to 350°. Melt butter in 8 x 13 inch pan in oven. Dip veal in 1/3 cup of the milk. Roll in mixture of 2 tablespoons Parmesan cheese, flour, salt and pepper. Put in pan. Bake uncovered for 30 minutes at 350°. Mix remaining milk and cheese. Pour tomato sauce around veal. Spoon cheese mixture on veal. Bake for 20 to 25 minutes longer. 4 servings.

PORK TENDERLOIN WITH SAUCE

4 to 6 pork tenderloin steaks
1 (6 oz.) carton sour cream
1 can consommé
onion flakes or chopped onion

Brown tenderloin slightly in butter or margarine. Mix together sour cream, consommé and onion and pour over tenderloins. Simmer on low heat for 45 minutes to 1 hour. (Good severed with potatoes or rice.)

BARBECUED MEAT LOAF

1 lb. ground beef
(Can use 1 1/2 lbs. hamburger, but
*   the pork adds flavor)*
1 medium onion, chopped
salt and pepper to taste
dash of Worcestershire sauce
dash of Kikkoman soy sauce
Sauce:
*   1/2 cup ketchup*
*   2 tablespoons prepared mustard*
*   2 tablespoons brown sugar*
*   2 tablespoons vinegar*

1/4 lb. ground pork
1 egg, slightly beaten
1 cup bread crumbs
1 green pepper, chopped

Mix meat, egg, bread crumbs, onion, green pepper and seasoning. Mix with your hands. Put into loaf pan and shape into loaf. Mix sauce and pour over loaf. Bake at 350° covered for 1 hour, basting occasionally. Bake uncovered for 20 to 25 minutes or until meat loaf is brown and sauce is thick. (This is my family's favorite.)

BURGUNDY MEAT BALLS

1 to 1 1/2 lbs. ground chuck beef
3 tablespoons onion, finely chopped
1 egg, lightly beaten
3/4 cup evaporated milk
dash of Worcestershire sauce
1 can beef broth or consommé,
*   undiluted*

1 teaspoon salt
pepper to taste
1/2 cup chopped celery
3/4 cup dry bread crumbs
3 tablespoons oil
1/2 cup Burgundy wine
1/2 cup plain flour

In a medium bowl combine beef, bread crumbs, milk, egg, onion, celery, salt and pepper. Mix well with hands and shape into 1 inch balls. Heat oil in large skillet. Roll meat balls in flour and brown well on all sides in oil. Remove and set aside. Sift a little flour into fat in skillet, brown lightly. Gradually blend in consomme' and wine. Cook until slightly thickened, stirring often. Return meat balls to skillet and simmer covered for 30 minutes. Serve over rice, noodles or potatoes. (You will agree these are the most delicious meat balls you ever tasted!} (Make small meat balls and serve in chafing dish for a party.)

BARBECUE ON BUNS
OR SLOPPY JOE'S

1 lb. ground beef
1/4 cup ketchup
1/3 cup chopped celery
1 tablespoon prepared mustard
1/2 teaspoon paprika
pepper to taste

1 can tomato paste
1/3 cup chopped onion
1/2 cup water
1/2 teaspoon chili powder
1/2 teaspoon garlic salt

Brown beef, onions and celery in small amount of fat. Combine with remaining ingredients. Simmer uncovered for 20 minutes or until desired consistency. Spoon on hamburger buns.

HAM LOAF

1 1/2 lbs. ground ham
1/4 lb. ground pork
1/4 lb. lean ground beef
1 1/2 dozen crackers, crushed
1 teaspoon Worcestershire sauce

2 eggs
1 1/2 cups milk
salt and pepper to taste

Mix all ingredients and shape with hands into a loaf. Bake in a loaf pan at 300° for 1 1/2 hours. Serve with mustard sauce.

Mustard Sauce

1 cup brown sugar, packed
3 eggs, beaten
1 tablespoon flour

1 cup water
1 cup vinegar
1/4 cup prepared mustard

Mix ingredients for sauce and cook in top of double boiler until thick, stirring constantly. Serve with ham loaf. You can pass it in a gravy boat and let each person help himself. (This is really tasty and delicious!)

HAMBURGER STROGANOFF

1/2 cup minced onions
1 clove garlic, minced
1 lb. ground beef
1 can cream of chicken soup, undiluted
2 tablespoons flour
1 (8 oz.) can mushrooms, sliced
2 tablespoons parsley, minced

1/4 cup butter
1 cup sour cream
2 teaspoons salt
1/4 teaspoon pepper
1/4 teaspoon paprika

Sauté onion and garlic in butter (or margarine) over medium heat. Add meat and cook red out. Add flour and seasonings and mushrooms. Cook for 5 minutes. Add soup, simmer uncovered for 10 minutes. Stir in sour cream. Heat through but do not boil. Sprinkle with parsley. Serve over noodles or rice. (This is an easy, delicious way to prepare stroganoff.)

EASY SWISS STEAK

1 1/2 lbs. round steak, 1 inch steak
1 envelope onion soup mix
2 tablespoons butter or margarine
1/2 lb. fresh mushrooms or 2 (4 oz.) cans mushrooms

Dot the center of 2 1/2 ft. of heavy wide aluminum foil with 1 tablespoon of the butter. Shake half of the onion soup mix on the foil (be sure the soup mix is evenly mixed). Over this place the steak, top with remaining soup mix, 1 tablespoon butter and mushrooms. Bring foil up and seal tightly. Place in shallow baking pan and bake at 350° for 1 to 1 1/2 hours. (You can also prepare pot roast by this recipe.)

GLAZE FOR BAKED HAM

1/2 cup honey   *1 cup brown sugar*
1/2 cup orange juice

Mix together. The last 30 minutes of baking, score ham fat. Avoid making scores too deep. It's a good idea to pour fat drippings from pan before pouring glaze over ham. Then when you baste with glaze it won't be diluted. Pour glaze mixture over ham. Continue baking about 30 minutes or until ham is well glazed.

OVEN BAKED PORK BARBECUE

6 to 7 lb. pork shoulder   *1 bottle Liquid Smoke*
2 medium onions, sliced   *salt and pepper to taste*
tabasco sauce to taste   *barbecue sauce*

Making slices 1 inch apart, slice across the port shoulder (don't cut quite through meat). Stuff with sliced onions. Pour 1/2 bottle Liquid Smoke over shoulder and sprinkle with salt and pepper. Wrap tightly in foil and bake at 300° for 6 hours. When cool enough to handle, but still warm, shred with a fork. Reheat to serve and add your own or bottled barbecue sauce, hot or mild to suit your taste. (This is an easy recipe and has a great smoked flavor.)

MINUTE STEAK PARMESAN

1 egg   *2 tablespoons water*
1 cup grated Parmesan cheese   *Dash of pepper*
5 beef cube steaks (about 4 oz. each)
1 cup finely crushed saltine crackers
1/2 cup cooking oil
1 (8 oz.) can pizza sauce

Beat together egg, water and pepper. Combine crumbs and half the cheese. Dip steaks in egg mixture, then in crumbs. In skillet, brown steaks in hot oil. Drain. Arrange steaks in a 10 x 6 x 1_ inch baking dish, cover with pizza sauce and sprinkle with remaining cheese. Bake at 325° for 20 minutes. (Tasty)

HAM (Tastes like Country Ham)

Center cut ham slices, 1/4 inch thick
1 tablespoon Worcestershire sauce
1/4 cup vinegar
1 tablespoon ketchup

Put ham slices in roaster and cover with sauce. Cover and cook at 300° until tender. Sprinkle brown sugar on top and place uncovered under broiler. Watch carefully. Cook until it browns slightly. (Makes plain tenderized ham taste like country ham.)

LEG OF LAMB

Generously salt and pepper lamb. Smear prepared mustard all over lamb. Sprinkle a little flour over all. Place a few pieces of garlic on the roast if desired. Sprinkle with Worcestershire sauce. Roast uncovered at 325° until it reaches desired doneness, about 20 minutes per lb. for a pink roast.

COUNTRY HAM

Soak ham in water to cover for 24 hours. Pour off water and then cover with more water. Put on stove and barely let water bubble, not really boil for 25 minutes to the pound. Add to the water 2 cups brown sugar, 1 cup vinegar, also a handful of whole cloves (add after it has cooled for a while). Let stand in water until completely cool. Skin and trim fat to 1/4 inch or less. Then press whole peppercorns all over top. (This is the best way to cook country ham, absolutely delicious!)(This recipe came from a friend in Kentucky.)

GOURMET PORK CHOPS

6 loin pork chops 1/2 inch thick
2 tablespoons flour
dash of pepper
1/4 teaspoon rosemary
1 (3 1/2 oz.) can French fried onion rings
1 teaspoon salt
3/4 cup water
1/2 cup sour cream
1 can mushroom soup

Trim fat from chops and heat in skillet until 2 tablespoons fat collect. Coat chops in flour, salt, pepper. Brown in hot fat. Place in baking dish. Combine soup, water, and rosemary. Pour over chops. Sprinkle with half of the onion rings. Cover. Bake at 325° for 45 to 50 minutes. Uncover: Sprinkle with rest of onion rings; bake 10 minutes. Remove to platter. Blend sour cream in soup mixture. Heat and serve with chops. Serves 6.

CORNISH HENS

Split hens in half if they are large. Salt and pepper to taste. Mix equal amounts of prepared mustard and melted butter. Smear all over each half. Put each half in a square of foil. Seal each square of foil well. Bake at 350° for approximately 1 hour. Test for doneness. Open foil and let brown for 5 or 10 minutes. Put juice aside. Put some juice over hens. Use rest of juice to serve over rice. (These are tasty and easy.)

SOUR CREAM AND DILL CHICKEN

8 to 10 chicken pieces, skinned
1 can cream of mushroom soup
1/2 can water
1 envelope dry onion soup mix
1 cup (8 oz.) sour cream
1 tablespoon lemon juice
1 teaspoon dill weed

Place chicken in a single layer in a 9 x 13 inch baking dish or pan. Combine rest of ingredients. Spoon mixture over chicken. Bake uncovered at 350° for 1 hour, turning chicken a few times until chicken is tender. Serve over rice.

Ramsey - Pomarede

CASSEROLES

SCALLOPED OYSTERS

1 1/2 pints fresh oysters (can use canned)
8 tablespoons butter, melted   pepper
2 cups saltine cracker crumbs   1/4 teaspoon salt
1 cup half and half (light cream)
1/2 teaspoon Worcestershire sauce

Drain oysters. Save the liquid from oysters. Butter a shallow baking dish. Pour the melted butter over the cracker crumbs. Toss lightly with a fork. Spread 1/3 of the crumbs on bottom of baking dish. Cover with half the oysters. Sprinkle with pepper. Layer another 1/3 of the crumbs and rest of oysters. Sprinkle with pepper. Combine oyster liquor with enough half and half to make 1 cup liquid. Add salt and Worcestershire sauce. Pour over casserole. Top with remaining crumbs. Bake at 350° for 30 minutes.

SEAFOOD CASSEROLE

1 lb. fresh boiled and deveined shrimp
   or 1 (6 oz.) can shrimp, deveined
2 cans crabmeat   1/2 cup milk
2 cans cream of mushroom soup   1/2 cup salad dressing
1 (5 oz.) can water chestnuts,   1 cup diced celery
   drained and sliced   dash of tabasco
2 tablespoons chopped parsley   1 green pepper, chopped
1 small can pimentos, chopped   2 teaspoons grated onion
2 cups cooked rice (regular not minute rice)
1 cup grated cheddar cheese

Combine soup, salad dressing and milk. Mix in shrimp, crabmeat and rest of ingredients except cheese. Put in a 2 quart, lightly buttered casserole. Sprinkle cheese on top. Bake at 350° for 30 minutes. Serves 8 to 10. (I sometimes put this in the individual sea shells and bake it in them, then serve in them.)(Nice for a luncheon this way.)(This is tasty if you like seafood.)

SCALLOPED CORN AND OYSTERS

1/4 cup finely chopped celery
1 cup frozen condensed oyster stew, thawed
   or 1 can oyster stew
1 cup milk   1/4 teaspoon salt
1 (1 lb.) can (2 cups) cream style corn   1 slightly beaten egg
1 1/2 cups medicum cracker crumbs   dash of pepper
2 tablespoons butter, melted   1/2 cup cracker crumbs

Combine celery, oyster stew, corn, 1 1/2 cups cracker crumbs, milk, egg, salt and pepper. Pour into 1 1/2 quart casserole (greased). Mix butter and 1/2 cup cracker crumbs. Sprinkle on top. Bake at 350° for 45 minutes to 1 hour or until knife inserted comes out clean. (This is a good combination of flavors.)

EASY RICE CASSEROLE

1 stick butter or margarine
1 medium size onion, finely chopped
1 cup plus 2 tablespoons uncooked regular rice
1 cup chicken broth
1 (10 oz.) can condensed beef bouillon or consommé
1 tablespoon Worcestershire sauce
1/2 teaspoon pepper
1/2 teaspoon salt
1 can sliced mushrooms, drained

Melt butter in skillet. Add onion and rice. Sauté, stirring for 5 minutes. Add remaining ingredients, and bring to a boil. Place in greased 1 quart casserole, cover, and bake at 350° for 1 hour. (Rice will take up all liquid.) Yield 5 to 6 servings. (This is so good served with beef or chicken.)

HASH BROWN POTATO CASSEROLE

2 pound package frozen hash brown potatoes, thawed
1/2 cup melted margarine
1/4 to 1/2 teaspoon salt
1/2 cup chopped onion
1 pint sour cream
1 can cream of chicken soup, undiluted
2 cups grated cheese

Topping:
  2 cups crushed corn flakes
  1/4 cup melted margarine

Mix all ingredients except topping. Be sure hash browns are thawed. Bake in greased long pyrex or 9 x 13-inch pan at 350° for 30 minutes or until bubbly. The last 10 minutes, put corn flakes and melted margarine (1/4 cup) on top. (Super and easy!) (Instead of frozen hash brown potatoes, you can cook your own potatoes. Peel and cube 8 medium potatoes and cook until just done but not mushy and continue as recipe states.)

BROCCOLI CASSEROLE

2 packages frozen chopped broccoli
3-4 green onions
1 tablespoon flour
1 can mushroom soup, undiluted
1 stick margarine
salt & pepper to taste
1 roll garlic cheese
1/4 cup milk

Cook broccoli and drain. Melt margarine, add onions, flour, seasoning, cheese, milk and soup. Mix with broccoli in lightly greased casserole. Top with cracker crumbs. Bake at 350° for 20 to 25 minutes. (This is one of the best broccoli casseroles you ever tasted!)

CABBAGE CASSEROLE

4 cups grated cabbage (use medium grater)
1 cup water chestnuts, sliced
1 can cream of celery soup
3/4 cup grated cheddar cheese

1/2 cup mayonnaise
1 small onion, chopped

Topping:
    1/2 cup melted margarine
    2 cups crushed corn flakes

Cover cabbage with mild salt water. Let stand 10 minutes and drain. Rinse and squeeze water out. Put cabbage in a well greased 9 x 13 inch baking dish. Drain and slice chestnuts and spread on cabbage. Mix together the celery soup, mayonnaise, chopped onion and cheese. Spread on cabbage and chestnuts. Put topping on. Bake in a 350° oven for 20 minutes or until brown. (Very tasty casserole.) (Even if you don't like cabbage, you'll like this.)

CHEESE STRATA

10 slices of bread, buttered
2 1/2 cups milk
1 tablespoon Worcestershire

4 eggs
5 slices sharp cheese

Remove crusts from bread, butter, and make into 5 sandwiches with the cheese. Cut each sandwich in half, fit them into a well-buttered oblong flat pyrex dish. Mix milk with beaten eggs and pour over the sandwiches. Put in refrigerator for 5 to 6 hours or overnight. Bake at 350° for 45 minutes or until puffed and brown. Serve at once. Serves 8 to 10. (This is a delicious, easy way to make cheese soufflé.)

CHEESE GRITS SUPREME

1 cup grits (quick cooking)
1/2 cup butter or margarine
1 roll garlic cheese or bacon cheese
1/2 cup cheddar cheese, grated

4 cups boiling water
3 eggs, beaten
2/3 cup milk

Cook grits in boiling water. When thick, add butter and garlic cheese or bacon cheese. Blend well, cool. Combine beaten eggs with milk. Stir into grits. Pour into greased 2-quart casserole. Sprinkle with grated cheddar cheese. Bake in a 325° oven for 35 to 45 minutes. Garnish with crisp curls of bacon. Serves 4 to 6. (So good served with ham or sausage.)

CREAMY POTATO CASSEROLE

8 medium potatoes, cut in 1-inch cubes
2 (3 ounce) packages cream cheese
1/4 cup chopped chives
   or green onions
1/2 cup melted margarine

1 (8 ounce) sour cream
1/4 teaspoon garlic salt
1/2 teaspoon salt
paprika

Cook potatoes in small amount of water; drain and mash. Beat cream cheese until smooth and add to potatoes. Add margarine, green onions and seasonings. Beat well and spoon into casserole. Sprinkle with paprika. Bake at 350° for 25 to 30 minutes.

CHEESE SQUASH CASSEROLE

6 yellow squash
3 tablespoons parsley flakes
1/2 stick butter or margarine
1 cup cheese Ritz cracker crumbs

1 onion, chopped
1/4 cup milk or cream
pepper to taste
Parmesan cheese

Cut up squash and onion and cook in small amount of water till done. Drain and mash. Add rest of ingredients, sprinkle Parmesan cheese on top. Bake in greased pyrex casserole at 350° for 25 to 30 minutes. (Tasty!)

BROCCOLI CASSEROLE

1 package frozen chopped broccoli
1/2 cup margarine
1/2 cup sharp cheese, grated
1/2 can mushroom soup, undiluted

1 whole egg
1 tablespoon grated onion
salt & pepper to taste

Cook broccoli and drain. Mix in all ingredients. Put in buttered casserole. Top with crushed crackers. Bake at 375° for 20 to 25 minutes. (Very tasty!)

(Remember when you use cheese in a recipe, usually no extra salt is needed.)

CHICKEN CASSEROLE

8 chicken breasts
2 cans cream of chicken soup
1 stick butter, melted

1 1/2 pints sour cream
2 tablespoons poppy seed
2 rolls Ritz crackers

Cook chicken breasts and cut up in chunks. Mix soup (undiluted), sour cream, and poppy seed. Crush Ritz crackers and mix with melted butter. Use a 9 x 13-inch pyrex. Put soup mixture (1/3) on the bottom, then layer of chicken, then Ritz crackers. Repeat layers with Ritz crackers on top, repeat the third time. Bake at 350° until bubbly. (Luscious!)

CORN PUDDING

1 can cream style corn
1/2 cup milk
3 tablespoons sugar
3 tablespoons butter (melted in
   baking dish)

1/2 cup coffee cream
3 eggs
3 tablespoons flour
1 tablespoon vanilla
(yes, 1 tablespoon)

Beat eggs with fork. Beat in sugar and flour (mixed together). Beat in corn, milk, cream, and vanilla. Melt butter in 8-inch square pan or pyrex. Pour egg and corn mixture into buttered pan. Bake at 325° for 50-60 minutes. (You can double this by using 1 can cream corn and 1 can whole grain corn (drained) and use a 9 x 13-inch dish or pan.)

CHICKEN TETRAZZINI

6 chicken breasts or a hen, cooked and cut
3 1/2 cups chicken broth
2 cups regular rice
2 cups chopped green pepper
5 ribs celery, chopped
1 medium onion, chopped
2 cans cream of mushroom soup
1 soup can milk
1 can sliced water chestnuts (8 oz.) drained
salt, pepper and thyme to taste

Cook rice with chicken broth, green peppers, celery and onion. Mix cut up chicken with rice and vegetables. Mix in mushroom soup and milk and water chestnuts. Season to taste. Spoon into 1 long (9 x 13-inch) casserole plus 1 medium size casserole. Top with grated cheese. Bake at 350° for 25 to 30 minutes or until bubbly. (Can make day before and refrigerate. Before putting in oven pour a little more milk over casserole so it won't be dry.) (This is the best chicken tetrazzini I've ever tasted.)

PINEAPPLE CHEDDAR CASSEROLE

1 (20 ounce) can pineapple chunks
3 tablespoons sugar
1 1/4 cups grated cheddar cheese melted
1 1/2 cups crushed Ritz crackers

3 tablespoons flour
3 tablespoons butter,

Drain pineapple, reserving 3 tablespoons juice. Arrange pineapple on the bottom of a greased 1-1/2 quart casserole. Stir together flour and sugar and sprinkle over pineapple. Drizzle the reserved pineapple liquid over top with the cheddar cheese. Mix together the crushed crackers and melted butter and distribute over the cheese. Bake casserole, covered, in a 350° oven for 15 minutes. Uncover and bake 10 minutes longer. (Good served with meat.)

SWEET POTATOES DELUXE

2 cups cooked mashed sweet potatoes
1 cup sugar (white)
1/4 cup milk or light cream
3/4 stick butter

2 eggs
1 teaspoon vanilla
1/2 teaspoon cinnamon
1/2 teaspoon nutmeg

Topping:
3/4 cup crushed corn flakes
4 tablespoons melted butter

1/2 cup brown sugar
1/2 cup finely chopped nuts

Mix sweet potatoes with white sugar, eggs, milk, butter and spices and vanilla. Bake in a buttered casserole for 20 minutes at 350°. Add topping and bake 10 minutes more. (This is a delicious way to serve sweet potatoes.)

GRATED SWEET POTATO CASSEROLE

3 cups grated raw sweet potatoes
1 cup milk
2 eggs, beaten

1 cup sugar
1 stick butter, melted
1 teaspoon nutmeg

Peel sweet potatoes and grate. Add milk, sugar, eggs, well-beaten, melted butter and nutmeg. Mix thoroughly. Place in shallow greased casserole or an iron skillet. Bake at 350° for 1 hour to 1-1/2 hours. When it gets brown on top, stir and let get brown again. Repeat several times until all is caramelized and brown. (This is a very old, delicious recipe.)

SHRIMP SPAGHETTI

3 tablespoons shortening
1 teaspoon Worcestershire sauce
1 medium onion, chopped fine
1/4 cup chopped green pepper
2 cups shrimp, canned or fresh
1 cup grated cheddar cheese or fresh Parmesan

1/2 teaspoon salt
4 ounces spaghetti
2/3 cup sliced mushrooms
1 clove garlic, minced
2 1/2 cups canned tomatoes

Melt shortening. Add onion and green pepper and saute. Add garlic, mushrooms, tomatoes, seasonings and uncooked spaghetti. Cover and cook on low heat for 25 minutes. Add shrimp and cheese and cook 10 minutes longer. (Different)

EGGPLANT CASSEROLE

6 slices bacon
1 chopped green bell pepper
1 large eggplant, peeled
1/2 cup grated cheese

1 chopped onion
1 large can tomatoes
salt & pepper to taste
1/2 cup bread crumbs

Fry bacon until crisp. Use bacon fat to saute' onion and green pepper. Add tomatoes and simmer for 10 minutes. Cut eggplant in cubes and cook until tender. Cook for a few minutes with tomato mixture. Put in casserole. Crumble bacon on top. Sprinkle with cheese and bread crumbs. Bake at 350° for 25 to 30 minutes.

BAKED BEAN CASSEROLE

2 tbs bacon drippings
2 tbs chopped celery
1 pound ground beef
dash of Worcestershire sauce
1 medium can pork and beans

2 tbs chopped onion
1 clove garlic, chopped
salt & tabasco to taste
1/2 cup tomato ketchup

Saute' onion and celery in drippings. Add beef and cook all red out. Add other ingredients and put in casserole or bean pot. Bake at 350° for 35 to 40 minutes. Crumble cooked, drained bacon on top. (Makes a hit at a picnic.)

VEGETABLE CASSEROLE

1 can shoepeg white corn, drained
1 can French green beans, drained
1 can celery soup, undiluted
1 cup cheddar cheese, grated
1 package or roll of Ritz crackers

1 medium onion, chopped
8 ounce sour cream
1/2 cup slivered almonds
1 stick margarine, melted

Mix onion, soup, sour cream and cheese. Spoon on top of beans and corn in buttered casserole. Crush crackers. Melt margarine and combine with crackers. Add almonds. Sprinkle on top of casserole. Bake uncovered for 30 minutes at 350°. (This casserole always makes a hit.)

OLD FASHIONED SQUASH CASSEROLE

8 medium yellow crook neck squash
1 medium onion, chopped
2 eggs
3/4 stick butter or margarine
1 cup cubed Velveeta cheese
1 teaspoon Worcestershire sauce
salt & pepper to taste
3/4 cup cracker crumbs
(do not use much salt as cheese and crackers are salty)

Cook squash in small amount of water until tender, drain. Mash with a potato masher. Saute' onion in butter and add Velveeta cheese. Stir until cheese melts. Add Worcestershire sauce and seasoning. Take off heat and add cracker crumbs, beaten eggs and squash. Spoon into 1-1/2 quart casserole and sprinkle with cheddar cheese if desired. Bake at 350° until bubbly. Serve immediately.

EASY CHILI

1 1/2 pounds ground lean hamburger meat
1 teaspoon salt
1 green pepper, chopped
1 can tomato soup + 1 can water
1 can tomato sauce

1 medium onion, chopped
1 garlic clove, chopped
chili powder to taste
2 cans red kidney beans

Cook hamburger meat in small amount of bacon fat, add salt. Add rest of ingredients and chili powder to taste. Simmer for 1 or 2 hours.

HOT FRUIT CASSEROLE

1 medium can pineapple slices
1 medium can peach halves
1 medium can apricot halves, peeled
2 tablespoons flour
1/2 cup brown sugar, packed

1 medium can pear halves
1 medium can apple rings
1 stick butter
1 cup sherry wine

Cook flour, butter, sugar, and sherry over medium heat until sugar melts and ingredients are blended. Drain fruit, put in 2 quart casserole. Pour on sauce. Refrigerate overnight. Cook at 350° for 25 minutes. Serves 12. (Pretty if you put apple rings on top.)

CHICKEN AND DRESSING CASSEROLE

In a 2-1/2 quart buttered casserole, place 1/2 package Pepperidge Farm Herb Stuffing Mix, then a layer of cut or sliced chicken, 1/4 cup each of chopped onion, celery, and green pepper. Then mix 1 can mushroom soup with 2 cups chicken broth. Pour over all. Put rest of stuffing mix on top. Bake at 350° for 25 minutes. You can add 1/2 cup slivered almonds and bake 10 minutes more if desired.

GREEN BEAN CASSEROLE

1 small can mushrooms, drained
1 can cream of mushroom soup, undiluted
1 can French fried onion rings

3 strips bacon
salt to taste
2 cans whole green beans

Fry bacon and season beans with bacon drippings. Cook beans until seasoning has gone through. Mix all ingredients except onion rings and bacon. Put in greased casserole and heat at 375° for 15 minutes. Then crumble bacon on top and onion rings. Heat at 400° for 3 minutes.

CORN BAKE

Jiffy cornbread mix (8-1/2 ounce)
8 ounce sour cream
2 sticks melted butter or margarine
1 (16 ounce) can whole kernel corn
1 (16 ounce) can cream style corn

2 eggs
1 tablespoon flour

Mix all ingredients together. Pour into casserole. Bake at 350° for 30 to 40 minutes.

BAKED CHEESE APPLES

1 stick butter
3/4 cup sugar
3/4 cup plain flour

1 can apples (or fresh)
1/2 lb. Velveeta cheese

Cream sugar and butter. Stir in flour. Cut cheese into cubes. Stir into apples. Mix all together and put into a 9 x 10 inch casserole. Bake at 350° until brown on top. (Different and tasty side dish.)

SPAGHETTI CASSEROLE

1 1/2 pounds lean hamburger (or you can use 1 pound)
1 onion, chopped   *1 clove garlic, chopped*
1 can mushrooms, drained   *salt & pepper to taste*
* 1 jar (small) pimento cheese spread
2 cans Franco-American spaghetti (with tomato cheese sauce)
1/2 can of chow-mein noodles or rice noodles

Cook hamburger and onion and garlic in small amount of fat. Add rest of ingredients. Spoon into medium size casserole. Put crisp noodles over top. Bake at 350° for 25 to 30 minutes. (Children really like this!)

* If you can't find the pimento cheese spread, chop pimentos into cream cheese and Velveeta cheese, then season with a little Worcestershire sauce, a little vinegar and sugar.

BAKED CHICKEN SALAD

2 cups cubed cooked chicken   *1/2 cup chopped celery*
1 can water chestnuts, sliced thin   *1/2 teaspoon salt*
1/2 cup chopped blanched almonds   *2 tablespoons grated onion*
1/2 can cream of chicken soup   *1/2 cup mayonnaise*
(undiluted)   *2 tablespoons lemon juice*
3 hard-cooked eggs, mashed or grated *dash of cayenne pepper*
2 tablespoons chopped pimento   *2 cups crushed potato*
                                        chips

Combine all ingredients except potato chips. Toss lightly and spoon into a 1-1/2 quart greased casserole. Spread chips on top. Bake at 350° for 25 to 30 minutes. Garnish with paprika and parsley. (Good luncheon dish.)

MUSHROOM BREAKFAST CASSEROLE

2 1/4 cups seasoned croutons   *4 eggs, beaten*
1 1/2 pounds bulk pork sausage   *2 1/4 cups milk*
1 (10 ounce) can cream of mushroom soup, (undiluted)
1 (4 ounce) can sliced mushrooms, drained
3/4 teaspoon dry mustard
2 cups grated cheddar cheese
parsley sprigs

Spread croutons in a lightly greased 13 x 9 x 2-inch baking dish. Set aside. Cook sausage until browned, stirring to crumble, drain well. Sprinkle sausage over croutons. Combine eggs, milk, soup, mushrooms, and dry mustard. Mix well and pour over sausage. Cover and refrigerate at least 8 hours or overnight. Remove from refrigerator, let stand 30 minutes at room temperature. Bake uncovered at 325° for 45 minutes. Sprinkle cheese over top and bake an additional 10 minutes or until cheese melts. Garnish with parsley if desired. Serves 10. (Good for a brunch or breakfast.)

ARTICHOKE CHICKEN CASSEROLE

2 (14 ounce) cans artichoke hearts, drained
2 2/3 cups diced cooked chicken breasts
2 (10 1/2 oz.) cans cream of chicken soup, undiluted
1 cup mayonnaise
1 teaspoon lemon juice
1/2 teaspoon curry powder
1 1/4 cups grated sharp cheddar cheese
1 1/4 cups bread cubes
2 tablespoons butter, melted
1/2 cup chicken broth
1/2 cup white wine

Arrange artichoke hearts in a greased 9 x 13 inch casserole. Spread chicken on top. Combine soup, mayonnaise, lemon juice, curry powder, chicken broth and wine and pour over chicken. Sprinkle with cheese. Toss bread crumbs with butter and place on top. Bake at 350° for 25 minutes. Can be prepared in advance. Serves 8. (A delicious luncheon dish.)

SPINACH CASSEROLE

3 packages frozen chopped spinach
1 can mushroom soup, undiluted
1/2 cup sour cream
2 tablespoons lemon juice
salt, pepper, garlic powder to taste

1 pound fresh mushrooms
1 small onion, chopped
1/2 cup mayonnaise
1 tablespoon butter

Cook spinach and drain well. Saute' stems of mushrooms and onion in 1 tablespoon butter. Mix with mushroom soup, sour cream, mayonnaise, and seasoning. Spread over spinach in buttered casserole. Place tops of mushrooms on top of casserole. Bake at 350° for 25 to 30 minutes. (This is tasty—even people who don't like spinach like this.) (Be sure to squeeze all water from spinach.)

SAUSAGE CASSEROLE

1 pound pork sausage (hot)
2 cups milk
6 slices day old bread, buttered on each side
1/4 pound cheddar cheese, grated

2 eggs
1/4 teaspoon dry mustard

Cook sausage and drain. Combine milk, eggs, and mustard. Put buttered bread in casserole. Crumble layers of sausage and layers of grated cheese. Repeat layers, then pour milk mixture over all. Let set overnight in refrigerator. Cook at 375° for 25 to 30 minutes. Serves 6-8. (A favorite for brunch or breakfast.)

BROCCOLI RICE CASSEROLE

1 package (10 ounce) frozen chopped broccoli
1/2 cup uncooked rice   1/2 cup milk
3/4 stick butter or margarine   1 can mushroom soup
1 medium onion, chopped   salt & pepper to taste
dash of Worcestershire sauce
grated sharp cheese for topping

Cook broccoli according to directions on package until just tender, drain. Cook rice in 1 cup water (do not use Minute Rice). Saute' onion in butter until tender. Combine broccoli, rice, onion and seasonings. Dilute soup with milk and mix with broccoli-rice mixture. Sprinkle top with cheese or mix in. Bake at 350° for 20 to 30 minutes. Serves 6 (Great taste!)

CHICKEN-HAM CASSEROLE SUPREME

1/2 cup chopped onion   1/4 teaspoon pepper
1/2 teaspoon salt   1 1/4 cups milk
3 tablespoons plain flour   2 tablespoons dry sherry
1 (4 ounce) can sliced mushrooms, undrained
2 cups chopped chicken or turkey
1 (5 ounce) can water chestnuts, drained and sliced
1 cup chopped cooked ham
1/2 cup shredded Swiss cheese
1 cup soft bread crumbs
3 tablespoons melted butter or margarine

Saute' onion in 2 tablespoons melted butter until tender, but not brown. Blend in flour, salt and pepper. Gradually stir in milk. Cook over low heat, stirring until smooth and thickened. Add sherry, mushrooms, chicken, water chestnuts and ham, stirring well. Spoon mixture into a lightly greased shallow 2 quart casserole. Sprinkle mixture with cheese. Combine bread crumbs with 3 tablespoons melted butter and spoon over casserole. Bake at 375° for 30 minutes or until lightly browned.

Delicious way to use leftover chicken or turkey and ham.

LESEUR GREEN PEA CASSEROLE

1 lb. can LeSeur green peas, drained
1 (5 oz.) can water chestnuts, drained and chopped
1 can mushroom soup
1 medium onion, chopped
1 (2 oz.) jar chopped pimentos
1/2 pkg. Pepperidge Farm stuffing mix
1/2 stick butter or margarine, melted
1/2 cup sharp cheese, grated

Mix peas, water chestnuts, mushroom soup, onion and pimentos. Put into a lightly greased casserole. Combine stuffing mix, melted butter and cheese. Put on top of casserole. Bake at 400° for 20 minutes. (Delicious!)

ASPARAGUS CASSEROLE

1 can mushroom soup (10 1/4 oz.)
2 cans green asparagus (medium size)
3/4 cup liquid drained from asparagus
1/2 stick (1/4 cup) butter or margarine
1 tblsp Worcestershire sauce
1/2 lb. cheddar cheese (grated)
1 1/2 cups cracker crumbs
1/2 cup chopped toasted almonds

Combine butter, soup, liquid from asparagus, and cheese in saucepan. Heat until blended. Add seasoning and almonds. Alternate asparagus, sauce, and cracker crumbs in lightly greased casserole, making two layers of each. Bake at 350° for 25 or 30 minutes. (You can add hard-cooked eggs to this. Tasty company casserole!)

Ramsey- Pomarede

SALADS
AND
SALAD DRESSINGS

CHICKEN SALAD

Cook chicken until it falls off bones. If you cook a fryer or chicken breasts use 2 chicken bouillon cubes in water in which you cook chicken. Remove chicken from bones and cut up, not too fine. Squeeze a little lemon juice over chicken. Sprinkle generously with fresh onion salt. You can omit onion salt and chop up a little green onion. Toss all through chicken. Chop several ribs of celery (depending on amount of chicken). Chop peeled apple (apple gives it a delicious flavor). Add celery and apple to chicken. Add chopped blanched almonds or pecans if desired. Make old fashioned cooked dressing and home made mayonnaise. Toss all together with the two kinds of dressing. Season to taste. (I use a little more mayonnaise than cooked dressing.) Let set in covered container several hours or overnight in refrigerator for flavors to blend. Serve on lettuce or make sandwiches, using home made mayonnaise. (This is my own recipe I worked out from taste and from the way my mother always made it.)

SPICED PEACH SALAD

2 (3 oz.) packages orange jello
1/4 teaspoon ground cloves
2 cups boiling water
1 can (29 oz.) sliced peaches (cut up)
1/2 cup mayonnaise

1/2 cup sugar
1 teaspoon cinnamon
1 1/2 cups peach syrup
4 tablespoons vinegar
1/2 cup Cool Whip

Mix together jello, sugar, cloves and cinnamon. Add boiling water and stir until dissolved. Add syrup, peaches and vinegar. Mix well and refrigerate until set. Mix together Cool Whip and mayonnaise. Spread on top. Serves 10. (If you like spiced peaches you'll love this.)

CHRISTMAS SALAD

1 (3 oz.) package of raspberry jello
1/4 cup chopped nuts (optional)
1 (8 1/4 oz.) can crushed pineapple, drained
1 can (16 oz.) whole cranberry sauce
1 teaspoon port wine (optional)

1/2 cup cold orange juice
1 cup hot water

Dissolve jello in 1 cup hot water. Add orange juice. Chill until it starts to thicken. Add pineapple, cranberry sauce, nuts and wine. (Good for the holidays.)

LOW CALORIE DRESSING

1 cup cottage cheese (small curd)
2 teaspoons lemon juice
1 tablespoon chopped chives
Dash of paprika

1/2 teaspoon garlic salt
Dash of pepper
1/2 cup buttermilk

Mix and serve on salad greens.

CONGEALED SLAW

1 package (3 oz.) lemon jello
1/2 cup cold water
1/4 cup sour cream
1 1/2 cups grated cabbage
1/2 cup chopped celery
1/2 cup grated carrots
1/2 cup chopped green pepper

1 cup hot water
2 tablespoons vinegar
1/4 teaspoon salt
1/2 cup mayonnaise
2 tablespoons grated onion
1/2 cup radishes, sliced

Dissolve jello in hot water. Add cold water, vinegar, sour cream and mayonnaise. Beat with mixer or blender. Add vegetables. Pour in individual molds or in long pyrex dish.

HI-C FRUIT SALAD

1 can pineapple tidbits,
drained (20 oz.)
1 banana, sliced
1 cup pecans, chopped (optional)

1 can mandarin oranges,
drained (11 oz.)
1 red apple, chopped,
do not peel

Mix above ingredients and cover with glaze:

1 cup cherry flavor Hi-C drink
1 1/2 tablespoons cornstarch

1/4 cup sugar
Dash of cinnamon

Cook drink, sugar and cornstarch until thick. Add cinnamon and mix well. Cool and pour over fruit. Refrigerate (children love this.)

APRICOT NECTAR SALAD

1 (3 oz.) package lemon jello
1 (3 oz.) package orange jello
2 cans (12 oz. each) apricot nectar
1 medium (15 1/4 oz.) crushed pineapple, drained

1 teaspoon plain gelatin
1/4 cup cold water

Dissolve orange and lemon jello separately in hot apricot nectar and pineapple juice to make 2 cups liquid for each. Add plain gelatin dissolved in 1/4 cup cold water to hot orange jello. Add lemon jello, reserving about 1/2 cup for topping. When jello begins to thicken, add crushed pineapple (drained) and pour into long 9 X 13 inch pyrex dish. Let set until firm.

TOPPING

1 (8 oz.) package cream cheese
1/2 cup nuts, chopped (optional)
1 can mandarin oranges, drained
1/2 cup mayonnaise

1 cup whipping cream,
whipped
rest of lemon jello

Soften cream cheese and add mayonnaise, whipping cream, jello and nuts. Spread over the congealed first layer. Arrange mandarin oranges on top. (This is my own original recipe. It is delicious and pretty.) Serves 12 to 16. Keep refrigerated.

DELICIOUS SALAD

1 package (3 oz.) lime jello
2 packages (3 oz. each) lemon jello
1 (8 1/4 oz.) can crushed pineapple,
   not drained
1 can sweetened condensed milk (Eagle Brand)

2 1/2 cups boiling water
1 cup nuts, chopped
1 small carton sour cream

Dissolve jello in boiling water. When jello begins to thicken add other ingredients. Pour into long pyrex dish on a 9 X 13 inch pan. Refrigerate. (Almost like dessert.)

APRICOT SALAD

1 package (3 oz.) orange jello
2 cups apricot nectar, heated (you can finish out apricot nectar with
   pineapple juice)
1 can (15 1/4 oz.) pineapple chunks, drained
1 can (17 oz.) apricots, drained and cut
1/2 cup chopped pecans, optional
1/2 cup maraschino cherries, cut

Dissolve jello in hot juice. When it begins to thicken, add other ingredients. Pour into molds or a square pyrex dish. Serves 8 or more.

BING CHERRY COCA-COLA SALAD

1 (3 oz.) package cherry jello
1 cup pecans, chopped
1 (3 oz.) package lemon jello
2 bottles (10 oz. each) Coca-Cola
1 (15 oz.) can pitted black cherries, drained
1 (8 1/4 oz.) can crushed pineapple, undrained

Dissolve jello in hot pineapple. Add Coca-Cola and put in refrigerator to thicken. When it is slightly thickened add drained cherries and nuts. Return to refrigerator to congeal completely. (Serve with cream cheese dressing.)

ASPARAGUS SALAD

1 can asparagus soup, undiluted
1 package (8 oz.) cream cheese
1/2 cup water
3/4 cup chopped celery
1/2 cup chopped green pepper

1 (3 oz.) package lime
   jello
1/2 cup mayonnaise
1 tablespoon grated onion
1/2 cup chopped nuts,
   optional

Mix water with soup and heat to boiling. Remove from heat and add jello, stir until dissolved. Add cream cheese and mayonnaise and blend in blender until smooth. Stir in remaining ingredients, turn into individual molds or a square pyrex dish. Chill until firm. Serves 8.

Always rinse individual salad molds with cold water and they will come out of molds easier.

Oil Dressing:

3 quarts of oil to 1 part of vinegar or lemon juice plus salt and pepper and other seasoning if desired.

Bacon Dressing:

Hot bacon drippings replace the oil in the basic oil dressing. Omit salt. This is especially good on cabbage, spinach or lettuce.

HAWAIIAN SALAD

1 envelope plain Knox gelatin	1/4 cup cold water
1/2 cup sugar	1 cup hot pineapple juice
1 cup crushed pineapple, drained	2 tablespoons lemon juice
1 cup orange sections, cut	1/4 teaspoon salt

Soften gelatin in cold water. Add sugar, salt, and hot pineapple juice. Stir until dissolved. Add lemon juice and juice from oranges. Cool and when it begins to thicken, add fruit. Turn into molds and serve with cream cheese dressing (you can use lemon jello and omit sugar.)

CREAM CHEESE DRESSING

1 (3 oz.) package cream cheese	1/2 cup whipping cream,
1/2 cup mayonnaise	whipped
1/2 cup finely chopped nuts	

Mash cheese, blend with mayonnaise, then add whipped cream and nuts. Serve on Hawaiian Salad or any fruit congealed salad. (Delicious.)

BLEU CHEESE DRESSING

1 cup salad oil	1/4 teaspoon pepper
3 tablespoons red wine vinegar	1/4 teaspoon paprika
1 clove garlic, minced	1/2 teaspoon celery salt
1 tablespoon Worcestershire sauce	1 tablespoon lemon juice
1 teaspoon prepared horseradish	
4 oz. bleu cheese, crumbled	

Mix all ingredients except bleu cheese together. Then gradually blend in bleu cheese. This should be made at least 8 hours in advance. Keeps in refrigerator for weeks in a covered jar. Yield 1 1/2 cups. (Good on a lettuce or combination salad.)

EASY FRUIT SALAD DRESSING

2 eggs
1/2 cup honey
1 cup miniature marshmallows

1/4 teaspoon salt
1 cup fresh lemon juice
1/2 pint sour cream

Mix eggs and salt in sauce pan. Combine lemon juice and honey, add slowly to egg mixture, stirring until smooth. Cook over low heat until it is like soft custard. Remove from heat, add marshmallows, stir until melted. Cool. Fold in sour cream. Makes 1 1/2 cups.

POPPY SEED DRESSING

1/2 cup sugar
1/2 teaspoon salt
1/3 cup red wine vinegar
1 tablespoon poppy seed

1 teaspoon dry mustard
1 tablespoon grated onion
1 cup oil

Mix red wine vinegar, sugar, dry mustard, salt, and grated onion in a blender. Blend and slowly add oil. Refrigerate. When ready to use add 1 tablespoon poppy seed. (This dressing is delicious on fruit.)

THOUSAND ISLAND DRESSING

3 cloves garlic, chopped fine
1/4 cup chili sauce
1 teaspoon prepared mustard
1 teaspoon Worcestershire sauce
Salt to taste
1 teaspoon black pepper

1 cup mayonnaise
1/4 cup ketchup
1/2 cup Wesson oil
1 teaspoon paprika
Dash of tabasco sauce
1 grated onion (small)

Juice of 1 lemon mixed with 1 tablespoon water

Mix all ingredients together in mixer or blender. (Makes a little over 1 pint. Keeps indefinitely in refrigerator.) (Really good on a green combination salad.)

FRENCH DRESSING

1 cup Wesson Oil
2 tablespoons Worcestershire sauce
2 tablespoons prepared mustard
1 clove garlic, minced
1 can condensed tomato soup, undiluted

1/2 cup vinegar
1/4 teaspoon salt
1 teaspoon pepper
1/4 cup sugar
1 large onion, grated

Mix all ingredients together and beat well. Pour into jar (quart). (Keeps indefinitely in refrigerator. Shake well before using.) (This is the best French dressing!)

MAYONNAISE (BLENDER)

1 egg or 2 egg yolks
1/2 teaspoon sugar
1/4 teaspoon salt
1 cup oil

2 tablespoons lemon juice
or vinegar
1/4 teaspoon dry mustard

Grind egg, lemon juice, sugar, salt and dry mustard for 70 seconds, adding oil in a steady stream through opening in top while motor is running. Makes 1 1/2 cups.

OLD FASHIONED COOKED DRESSING

1/4 cup sugar
1 teaspoon salt
2 teaspoons dry mustard
4 slightly beaten egg yolks
1/2 cup vinegar

1/4 cup flour
Dash of cayenne pepper
1 1/2 cups milk
1 tablespoon butter

Mix dry ingredients, add egg yolks and milk. Cook in top of double boiler until thick, stirring constantly. Add butter (or margarine). Add vinegar, a little at a time, stirring all the time. Mix well and cool. Makes 2 1/2 cups. (This is delicious in potato salad and chicken salad mixed with mayonnaise.)

7-UP LEMON SALAD

2 small (3 oz.) boxes of lemon jello dissolved in 2 cups boiling water. Cool and add 2 cups 7-Up drink. Add 3 bananas, sliced and 1 can (15 1/4 oz.) crushed pineapple, drained (save juice).

Stir all ingredients together in large bowl or in a long pyrex dish. Chill overnight or several hours.

Top with cooked dressing or topping:

1 cup pineapple juice
1/2 cup sugar
1 heaping cup of Cool Whip

2 tablespoons flour
1 egg

Blend pineapple juice, flour, sugar and egg in heavy saucepan and cook until thick, stirring often. When cool add Cool Whip or whipped cream. Blend well and spread over congealed salad. When ready to serve sprinkle on top with grated sharp cheese. (A delicious, refreshing salad.)

FROZEN STRAWBERRY SALAD

1 pint strawberries (can use frozen but drain most of juice off)
2 small packages (3 oz. each) or 1 large package cream cheese
1 pint whipping cream
16 marshmallows
1/2 cup mayonnaise or salad dressing
1 (20 oz.) can crushed pineapple, drained
1 cup pecans, chopped

Sweeten strawberries and let stand until juice is drawn out. Let marshmallows soak in drained pineapple. Mix strawberry juice with creamed cheese. Whip cream. Mix all ingredients together. Freeze in 9 x 13 inch pan or pyrex. (This is a delicious frozen salad.)

CRANBERRY FRUIT SALAD

2 1/2 envelopes plain gelatin
1 1/2 cups sugar
1 cup chopped apples (unpeeled)
1 can mandarin oranges (11 oz.)
1 cup chopped cranberries

2 cups cranberry juice
1/2 cup lemon juice
1/2 cup seedless grapes
halved
1/2 cup chopped nuts

Sprinkle gelatin over 1 cup cranberry juice in saucepan, let stand 5 minutes to soften. Stir over low heat until gelatin dissolves. Add sugar to hot juice mixture and stir to dissolve. Pour into large bowl, add remaining cup of cranberry juice and lemon juice. Chill until it begins to thicken. Have fruit and nuts prepared and mix with thickened juice. Pour into mold sprayed lightly with Pam. Let refrigerate overnight. (This is a different, delicious cranberry salad.)

RAW CRANBERRY SALAD

1 cup cranberries, ground or chopped
fine in food processor
1/2 cup sugar
1 (8 oz.) can crushed pineapple
1 apple, ground or chopped with cranberries

1 (3 oz.) package lemon
jello
1 cup orange juice
1/2 cup boiling water

Sweeten cranberries and apple with 1/2 cup sugar. Let stand in refrigerator for several hours or overnight. Dissolve jello in water and orange juice heated to boiling. When it begins to thicken add cranberry apple mixture and crushed pineapple juice and all. Pour into molds. (You can add nuts to this if desired.)

To hold up congealed jello salads, use 1 teaspoon of plain gelatin, softened in a little cold water, then mix it with the hot liquid when you dissolve jello.

SPINACH SALAD

1 1/2 lbs. fresh spinach	*1/4 lb. fresh mushrooms*
4 hard-cooked eggs, chopped	*8 strips of bacon, crisply fried and crumbled*

Wash spinach and remove stems. Tear into pieces. Slice mushrooms very thin lengthwise.

Dressing:

5 tablespoons red wine vinegar	*1 cup oil (not olive oil)*
4 tablespoons sour cream	*1 teaspoon salt*
2 tablespoons sugar	*2 cloves garlic, crushed*
2 teaspoons chopped parsley	*1/2 teaspoon dry mustard*
Coarsely ground black pepper	

Mix dressing in blender, pour oil slowly through hole into other ingredients. Mix a few hours before using. Toss spinach and mushrooms with desired amount of dressing; Top with eggs and bacon. (This is really tasty, and a change from a combination lettuce salad.)

BEET ASPIC

1 package lemon jello (3 oz.)	*1 cup boiling water*
1/2 cup beet juice	*1 tablespoon vinegar*
2 slices onion	*1/2 teaspoon salt*
1 tablespoon horseradish	*1 cup diced celery*
2 cups beets, diced or sliced	

Place jello in blender or food processor. Add boiling water. Cover and blend or chop for 3 seconds. Add remaining ingredients and blend until vegetables are coarsely cut. Chill until it begins to thicken and pour into molds.

SOUR CREAM POTATO SALAD

4 cups sliced or cubed cooked potatoes	*1/2 cup diced cucumbers*
1 onion, minced	*1/2 to 1 cup diced celery*
1 teaspoon celery seed	*Salt and pepper to taste*
3 hard-cooked eggs	*1/2 cup mayonnaise*
1 1/2 cups sour cream	*1 teaspoon prepared mustard*

Combine potatoes, cucumber, celery and onion. Blend. Cut egg whites into small pieces and add to potatoes. Mash yolks and combine with sour cream, mayonnaise, mustard, celery seed, salt and pepper. Blend with potato mixture. Serves 8 to 10. (A tasty, tart potato salad.)

KRAUT SALAD

1/2 cup chopped onion
1 medium size (16 oz) can
chopped kraut, drained

1/4 cup sugar
1/2 cup chopped celery

Mix and let stand for 5 hours before serving. (Good with meats.)

PINK ARCTIC FREEZE

2 (3 oz.) packages cream cheese
2 tablespoons mayonnaise
1 cup crushed pineapple or tidbits,
    drained
1/2 cup chopped nuts

2 tablespoons sugar
1 cup cream, whipped
2 cups whole cranberry
    sauce

Soften cream cheese, blend in mayonnaise and sugar. Add cranberry sauce, pineapple and nuts. Fold in whipped cream. Pour into a square pyrex dish. Freeze firm. Serves 8 to 10. (This is the best frozen salad!)

SHRIMP SALAD

2 packages frozen ready to cook
    shrimp (12 oz. size)
2 teaspoons prepared mustard
2 teaspoons thinly sliced celery
1/8 teaspoon pepper
1 tablespoon chopped parsley

1 cup mayonnaise
1 cup bottled Italian style
    dressing
1 teaspoon lemon juice
1 tablespoon grated onion

Cook shrimp according to package directions. Plunge into cold water, drain. In medium bowl pour Italian dressing over shrimp. Cover, refrigerate at least 1 hour, stirring several times. In small bowl combine mayonnaise, mustard, lemon juice, parsley, onion, pepper. Drain shrimp, add celery, toss with mayonnaise mixture. Serve on lettuce. Dust with paprika. Serves 6 to 8. (This is the best shrimp salad you ever tasted.)

STRAWBERRY SOUR CREAM SALAD

2 packages (3 oz. each) strawberry jello
2 cups boiling water
1 (15 1/4 oz.) can crushed pineapple
2 (10 oz.) packages frozen sliced strawberries
1 cup sour cream
3 large fully ripe bananas
1 tablespoon gelatin softened in 1/4 cup cold water

Dissolve jello in boiling water, add softened gelatin, add berries and stir until thawed. Add bananas that have been mashed. Add pineapple. Pour half of mixture in long pyrex dish. Chill until firm. Spoon sour cream over firm jello. Add rest of mixture and chill until firm. (A favorite, almost like dessert.)

FROZEN FRUIT SALAD

Dressing:
1/4 cup sugar
1 cup fruit juice
2 tablespoons vinegar

1 egg
2 tablespoons flour

Mix sugar and flour, beat egg, and add other ingredients. Cook until it thickens in top of double boiler. Cool and add:

1 cup diced pears
3 diced bananas
1 cup whipping cream, partially whipped

1 cup diced pineapple
1 dozen maraschino
cherries

Freeze in pyrex or in muffin tins lined with paper baking cups. (This is the old fashioned way to make frozen fruit salad. Delicious!)

FROZEN HONEY FRUIT SALAD

2 tablespoons sugar
1/2 cup honey
1 beaten egg
1 cup diced orange sections
1 small can pitted Bing cherries, quartered
1 cup whipping cream, whipped

1 tablespoon flour
1/3 cup lemon juice
1 ripe banana, sliced
1 (1 lb.) can fruit
cocktail, drained

In saucepan combine sugar, flour, and honey. Bring to boiling. Cook 1 minute, stirring constantly. Gradually stir lemon juice into egg, then add small amount of honey mixture, return to remaining mixture. Bring just to boiling, stirring constantly, remove from heat. Cool. Stir in fruits, fold in whipped cream. Pour into pyrex dish. Freeze until firm. Makes 6 to 8 servings. (This frozen fruit salad has an unusual tart flavor, different from most.)

ASHEVILLE SALAD

1 can tomato soup
2 tablespoons unflavored gelatin
2 tablespoons lemon juice
1 (3 oz.) package cream cheese
4 tablespoons mayonnaise
1 cup finely chopped celery
1 cup finely chopped pecans
2 tablespoons finely chopped green pepper (optional)
1/2 cup sliced stuffed green olives
Red pepper to taste

1 can water
1/2 cup cold water

Heat soup and water. Dissolve gelatin in cold water. Add to hot soup. Mix mayonnaise and softened cream cheese until creamy. Add to soup, stirring until well blended. Add remaining ingredients. Pour into ring mold or individual molds. Refrigerate until firm. Serves 10-12.

CRISP VEGETABLE SALAD

1 package lemon jello (3 oz.)
1 cup hot water
1 tablespoon vinegar

1 cup cold water
1 teaspoon salt

Mix together above ingredients. Chill until slightly thickened.

Fold in:
    3/4 cup diced or sliced cucumber
    1/2 cup thinly sliced red radishes
    1/2 cup thinly sliced green onions
    1/2 cup thinly sliced carrots

Pour into individual molds or a 1 quart mold. Chill until firm, overnight if possible. (Delicious with chicken and wild rice.)

RAW BROCCOLI SALAD

1 head broccoli flowerettes
1/2 lb. bacon, cooked and crumbled

2 red onions, sliced thin
1 cup grated cheese

Mix above ingredients with:

1 cup mayonnaise
1/4 cup sugar
1 tablespoon vinegar

Keeps well in refrigerator.

TOMATO ASPIC

1 (3 oz.) package lemon jello
1 cup chopped celery
Dash of red pepper
1/4 cup cold V-8 juice

2 cups V-8 juice heated
2 green onions, chopped
1 teaspoon plain gelatin
Small jar stuffed olives,
    sliced

Dissolve lemon jello in heated V-8 juice. Add plain gelatin which has been softened in 1/4 cup cold juice. Add chopped celery and green onions and red pepper. Let simmer for a few minutes. Let cool and add olives. Pour into square pyrex dish. Chill until firm. (Good served with chicken or tuna salad or cottage cheese.)

CURRIED SEAFOOD SALAD

1/2 cup mayonnaise
1 can chunk tuna, drained
1 cup shrimp
1/2 cup stuffed olives or ripe olives chopped

2 tablespoons lemon juice
1 teaspoon curry powder
1/2 cup chopped celery

Blend mayonnaise, lemon juice, and curry together. Add remaining ingredients and toss. Serve on lettuce or in avocado halves. Serves 4 to 6.

WILTED LETTUCE

5 slices bacon, diced
1/4 cup minced onion
1/2 teaspoon salt
2 tablespoons water
1 large head of lettuce,torn (home grown is best)

1 beaten egg
2 tablespoons sugar
1/3 cup cider vinegar

Cook bacon until crisp. Combine remaining ingredients, except lettuce, add to bacon and drippings. heat just to boiling, stirring constantly. Pour hot dressing over lettuce, toss lightly and serve at once.

CALICO MOLD

1 envelope plain gelatin
1 cup cold water
1 cup sour cream
4 oz. green chilies, drained
2 tablespoons chopped pimento
2 tablespoon chopped ripe olives
1 tablespoon chopped onion
Salt and pepper to taste

Soften gelatin in cold water. Dissolve softened gelatin over hot water, stirring until dissolved. Combine with all other ingredients stirring until well mixed. Put in lightly oiled mold. Refrigerate until ready to serve. If using a ring mold, serve with shrimp in the center. (Tasty and good to serve for a buffet.)

CRANBERRY SALAD

2 (3 oz.) pkgs. orange jello
1 (3 oz.) pkg. cherry jello
1/2 cup sugar
1 small (6 oz.) can orange juice concentrate
1 can whole cranberry sauce
1 large can crushed pineapple, drained
1/2 cup celery, chopped fine
1/2 cup nuts, chopped fine

Pinch of salt
1/2 cup pineapple juice
2 cups boiling water

Dissolve jello in boiling water and pineapple juice. Add sugar and stir well. When cool, add orange juice concentrate, undiluted. Stir well. Refrigerate and when it begins to thicken, add cranberry sauce, pineapple, celery and nuts. Pour into a 9 x 13 inch pyrex dish and refrigerate until ready to serve.

WALDORF SALAD

2 cups diced apples
1 tablespoon lemon juice
1/2 cup mayonnaise or salad dressing

1 cup chopped celery
1 cup chopped nuts
Raisins, if desired

Mix and chill thoroughly. Serve on lettuce.

Ramsey- Pomarede

VEGTABLES AND FRUITS

STUFFED MUSHROOMS

1 lb. large fresh mushrooms, remove stems and chop stems fine
1/2 onion, chop fine

2 teaspoons Worcestershire sauce   pinch of cayenne pepper
1/2 teaspoon white pepper   1/4 cup butter
1/4 teaspoon garlic powder   1/4 teaspoon salt
1 (4 oz.) can chopped clams   1 oz. Vermouth (optional)
1 teaspoon Kitchen Bouquet   1/2 cup sour cream
1 tablespoon chopped fresh parsley   3/4 cup fresh bread
                                             crumbs

Sauté onion and mushroom stems in butter or margarine until onions are translucent. Remove from heat and add remaining ingredients. Stuff caps of mushrooms with mixture. Hollow out caps enough to put in stuffing. Bake at 350° for 20 minutes. (These are luscious, wonderful for appetizers or main course.)

CARROT RING

2 cups cooked carrots, mashed   2 cups grated cheese
3 eggs   salt and pepper to taste
1/2 cup milk   1/4 cup butter, melted

Mix all ingredients together and spoon into a greased ring mold. Bake at 350° for 40 minutes or until knife inserted comes out clean. Turn out onto warm platter. Run knife around edges and put wet cloth on bottom of ring mold so it will turn out. Fill center with cooked green peas or lima beans. (This is so pretty and tasty.)

BLENDER HOLLANDAISE SAUCE

Melt 1/2 cup butter or margarine. Put 2 tablespoons fresh lemon juice, 4 egg yolks and 1/4 teaspoon salt in blender jar; blend briefly. Then on high speed add melted butter in a thin but steady stream. Serve on broccoli, asparagus or any vegetable (cooked).

CHEESE PUFFED IRISH POTATOES

3 medium size potatoes   1 teaspoon salt
2/3 cup hot milk   2 eggs, separated
2 tablespoons chopped pimento   1 cup grated cheddar
1/2 of 1 small onion, chopped   cheese
2 tablespoons butter or margarine

Cook potatoes and onions until tender. Drain, mash and add hot milk, egg yolks, salt, and butter. Last fold in cheese, pimento, and stiffly beaten egg whites. Bake at 350° for 25 minutes. Serve immediately. (The amount of milk depends on the kind of potatoes used.) (This is like a soufflé and is best served right out of the oven.)

FRIED OKRA

Cut okra in 1/2 inch circles, soak in buttermilk until ready to cook. Drain in colander. Dip okra in half plain corn meal and half plain flour mixed together with salt. Put enough oil in skillet to cover okra. Have oil hot, but not smoking. Keep okra separated while frying. Fry until golden brown. Drain well on paper towels. (This is a fool proof way to fry okra, always crisp and meal does not slide off. This even works for frozen okra.)

EASY WAY TO COOK CABBAGE

Shred a nice green head of cabbage, being careful not to cut too much of the hard, white stem with green part. Drop in boiling, salted water. Cover. Cook only 10 to 15 minutes (not mushy). Drain. Pour melted butter or margarine over cabbage, sprinkle with a little red pepper when you put in the serving dish.

STUFFED EGGPLANT

1 large firm eggplant (1 1/2 to 2 lbs.)

Slice off top on flat side. Scoop out center, being careful not to break through skin. Leave enough inside for a firm shell. Take out inside and cook in small amount of salted water, covered, until tender. Mash thoroughly. Add 6 crumbled soda or Ritz crackers, 1 small can chopped ripe olives (1/2 cup), 1 tablespoon bacon drippings in which 1 small green pepper, and 1 medium size onion, chopped have been sautéed until tender. Add a dash of celery salt and pepper and 1 can Hunt's tomato sauce. Mix all together and put back in shell. Bake for 20 minutes at 350° or until light brown and bubbly. (This is a tasty, different way to serve eggplant.)

MARINATED CARROTS or COPPER COINS

1 can condensed tomato soup
1 teaspoon Worcestershire sauce
3/4 cup vinegar
1 teaspoon prepared mustard
1 green pepper, cut in pieces
1 jar cocktail onions or chopped onion

1/2 cup salad oil
2/3 cup sugar
salt and pepper to taste
2 bunches carrots

Wash and scrape carrots and cut cross-wise. Cook until just tender. Drain and cool. Mix soup, oil, sugar, vinegar, mustard, and seasonings. Add carrots, green pepper, and onions to marinate and leave in refrigerator overnight before using. (This will keep a week or more in refrigerator.)

McMINNVILLE COLE SLAW

Select young tender green cabbage. Shred on medium grater and put in bowl with a little cracked ice on top. Keep in refrigerator for several hours to crisp. Make the following sauce:

1/3 cup apple vinegar
1/4 cup sugar
1 teaspoon celery seed
few drops onion juice

Do not use any salt as it weakens the "sweet sour" taste. Do not cook the sauce, just mix (cold) and stir until sugar is dissolved. Pour over the shredded cabbage and keep in the refrigerator until ready to serve. (Delicate and refreshing. Also delicious made with red cabbage.) This recipe came from an old Inn (the Sedberry Hotel) in McMinnville, Tennessee where President Andrew Jackson used to always spend a night when traveling (horseback) from Washington, D.C. to his home in Nashville.

CALIFORNIA STUFFED POTATOES

6 baking potatoes   *salt and pepper to taste*
2 tablespoons dry onion soup mix   *3/4 cup sour cream*
3/4 cup hot milk (amount of milk varies with kind of potatoes used)
butter or margarine for brushing

Preheat oven to 400°. Wash and thoroughly dry potatoes. Rub with Crisco shortening and bake until soft. Meanwhile combine the onion soup mix and sour cream. Cut a slice from the top of each potato. Scoop potato from each shell, being careful not to tear shell. Mash potatoes (I use mixer), gradually beat in hot milk, onion soup mixture, sour cream and salt and pepper (may not need much salt). Whip until fluffy in mixer. Spoon stuffing in each shell, rounding slightly. Brush with butter and brown in hot oven (425°) for 10 or 15 minutes. (Can put butter in potatoes when beating in mixer, and put cheese on top of each potato.) (Can prepare ahead, wrap each potato in foil and freeze.)

HOT SAUCE FOR BROCCOLI

1/2 stick butter or margarine   *1 cup mayonnaise*
2 tablespoons horseradish   *1/2 teaspoon salt*
1 teaspoon tabasco sauce   *1/2 teaspoon dry mustard*
1/4 teaspoon cayenne pepper   *1 onion, grated*

Stir all ingredients together in top of double boiler until well blended and hot. (This is also tasty on asparagus.)

STUFFED SQUASH

Select small yellow squash, cut off long ends and boil with whole squash until just tender. Slice off a little of top and scoop out inside. Mash ends and inside pulp with butter, salt, minced onion, cream of mushroom soup (undiluted), grated cheese, and a dash of Worcestershire sauce. Refill squash shells. Sprinkle cracker crumbs or bread crumbs on top. Dot with butter and bake in pan of shallow water at 350° until bubbly and light brown. (Can freeze before baking.)

BAKED APRICOTS

1 (16 oz.) box Ritz crackers   *1/2 cup butter*
2 (16 oz.) cans peeled apricots   *1 cup brown sugar (packed)*

Roll Ritz crackers to a fine meal. Drain apricots and remove seeds. Sprinkle layer of the cracker meal in bottom of 8 x 8 inch baking dish. Place layer of apricot halves on cracker meal. Cover apricots with layer of brown sugar. Dot with small bits of butter, then make another layer of all. Make last layer thin with cracker meal. Bake at 300° for 1 hour. (It should be thick and crusty on top.) Serves 6. (Unusual and delicious with meats.)

TOP OF STOVE BAKED APPLES

5 or 6 large, firm apples   *1 cup sugar*
1/4 teaspoon powdered cloves   *1/2 teaspoon cinnamon*
3 slices unpeeled orange   *1/3 cup water*
3 slices unpeeled lemon
extra sugar for glazing tops

Core apples, slice thin slice from bottom of each, and peel about 1/3 of the way down from top. Into large heavy skillet spread the cup of sugar. Add cloves, cinnamon, orange and lemon slices. Place apples top side down on the bed of sugar and pour water over them. Cover skillet tightly and steam on top of stove for about 15 minutes. Carefully turn apples over, replace cover and allow to cook for another 15 minutes (or until apples test done with a fork.) Remove lid. Sprinkle sugar over apples and place under broiler unit (not too close) for about 10 minutes, spooning syrup in bottom of skillet over the apples every minute or so, and adding more sugar if desired. The top of the apples should be candied, crisp and bubbly. Cool slightly and serve on a platter. (For a red color use a few cinnamon candies or red food color.)

CURRIED FRUIT

1 large (29 oz.) can peach halves
1 small can (17 oz.) apricots
1 large can (29 oz.) pears
3 small cans (8 1/4 oz. each) pineapple chunks
10 maraschino cherries
1/3 cup melted butter
4 teaspoons curry powder
3/4 cup brown sugar (packed)

Drain fruit well. Mix butter, brown sugar, and curry powder. Lay fruit in a shallow baking dish, hollow side up. Cherries on top. Dot all over with butter and sugar mixture. Bake at 325° for 1 hour basting frequently. Cool and refrigerate. Warm over at 350° for 30 minutes. Serves 10. (This is pretty and simple to make.)

BROCCOLI WITH LEMON SAUCE AND PECANS

1 (1 1/2 lb.) bunch fresh broccoli
3 tablespoons lemon juice
1 tablespoon corn starch
2 tablespoons melted butter or margarine

1 cup chicken broth
2 tablespoons sugar
1/4 teaspoon pepper
1/2 cup chopped pecans

Combine chicken broth, corn starch, and lemon juice in a small saucepan or in the top of a double boiler. Cook over medium heat, stirring constantly until thickened. Stir in sugar and pepper. Trim off large leaves of broccoli. Remove tough ends of lower stalks. Peel with a very sharp knife the stalks that are left. Soak in salted water. Then steam broccoli until crisp tender. Drain and arrange on serving platter. Spoon sauce over broccoli. Sauté pecans in butter until golden brown. You can adjust the amount of lemon juice to suit your taste. Sprinkle over broccoli before serving. Serves 6 to 8. (This is a gourmét way to serve broccoli — tasty and not high calorie.)

MARINATED VEGETABLES

3 ribs of celery, chopped or cut in thin strips
flowerettes from 1 bunch broccoli
1 head cauliflower, broken into pieces
3 grated carrots
1 small red onion, cut in thin slices or chopped
8 large mushrooms, sliced
Dressing:
3/4 cup vegetable oil
2 teaspoons dry mustard
2 tablespoons poppy seed
(optional)

1/2 teaspoon salt
1/2 cup vinegar
1/3 cup sugar

Marinate vegetables in dressing for at least 3 hours, overnight is better. Drain well before serving. (Keeps indefinitely in refrigerator.)

CREAMY LIMA BEANS

10 oz. pkg. Fordhook lima beans
2 tablespoons sliced green onions
*   with tops*
1/4 teaspoon salt
2 teaspoons brown sugar

1 tablespoon butter
1 tablespoon flour
dash of pepper
1/2 cup milk
1/2 cup sour cream

Cook limas according to package directions, drain. In medium saucepan, cook green onion in butter or margarine until tender, but not brown. Blend in flour, salt, and pepper. Add milk and brown sugar. Cook until thickened, stirring constantly. Stir sour cream and drained cooked limas into sauce mixture. Heat through, but do not boil. Serves 4. (A tasty way to serve limas.)

SOUTHERN OKRA

1 cup cut okra
1 medium onion, chopped
3 tomatoes, peeled and quartered
1 teaspoon flour (plain)
1/2 teaspoon pepper

1 green pepper, chopped
1/4 cup oil
1 teaspoon sugar
1/2 teaspoon salt

Cook onions and green pepper in oil. Add tomatoes and cook slowly for 5 minutes. Add okra and remaining ingredients. Cook over low heat until vegetables are just tender, stirring as little as possible.

Note: 1 cup canned tomatoes may be substituted in place of fresh tomatoes.

Serves 4. (This is so good served with black-eyed peas.)

APRICOT BAKED SWEET POTATOES

3 lbs. sweet potatoes
1 1/2 tablespoons corn starch
1/4 teaspoon cinnamon
1/2 cup hot water
2 teaspoons grated orange peel

1 cup brown sugar
1/4 teaspoon salt
1 cup apricot nectar
2 tablespoons butter
1/2 cup chopped pecans

Cook potatoes until tender but not mushy. Cool. Combine sugar, cornstarch, cinnamon, and salt in a medium saucepan. Stir in apricot nectar, hot water, and orange peel. Bring to a full boil stirring constantly. Remove from heat. Stir in the butter. Then stir in pecans. Cut peeled potatoes in half or in smaller pieces and place in a 7 1/2 x 12 inch baking dish. Pour sauce over potatoes so that all are glazed. (Cover and refrigerate overnight if desired.) Bake covered at 375° for 25 to 30 minutes or until sauce is bubbly. Freezes well. Serves 8. (Can make this a day ahead - delicious taste.)

REFRIGERATOR SLAW

2 large cabbage heads
2 sweet green peppers
3 large onions

Chop or shred above ingredients. Place in ice water for approximately 3 hours.

1 tablespoon white mustard seed	1 tablespoon salt
3 cups sugar	1 teaspoon tumeric
2 cups vinegar	1 teaspoon celery seed

Mix above ingredients and bring to a boil. Let cool. Mix with drained cabbage, peppers, and onions. Mix with hands. Keep in refrigerator. Keeps indefinitely.

BRANDY PEACHES

16 canned peach halves
1 cup firmly packed brown sugar
1/3 cup butter or margarine, melted
vanilla ice cream

1 cup maple syrup
ground cinnamon to taste
1/3 cup brandy

Place peach halves, cavity side up in a lightly greased 13 x 9 x 2 inch baking dish. Spoon about 1 tablespoon syrup, 1 tablespoon sugar, and 1 teaspoon butter into each cavity. Sprinkle lightly with cinnamon and bake uncovered at 325° for 20 minutes. Remove from the oven and pour brandy over peaches. Place each peach half in an individual serving dish and top with vanilla ice cream. Makes 16 servings.

MUSHROOMS IN SOUR CREAM

1 lb. mushrooms, wash and cut stems nearly to buttons
separated onion slices
fresh lemon juice
sour cream
butter or margarine

Melt margarine in skillet. Sauté onions until it begins to color. Stir in mushrooms, cover and cook over low heat about 8 minutes. When done add lemon juice and stir in sour cream.

ASPARAGUS AMANDINE

2 (10 oz.) pkg. frozen asparagus spears
1/3 cup butter or margarine
1/2 cup slivered blanched almonds
juice of 1/2 lemon

Sauté almonds in butter until golden, stirring occasionally. Add lemon juice. Cook asparagus by directions on package. Drain. Pour sauteed almonds over hot asparagus. (Can use fresh asparagus. Also good with green beans.)

GLAZED SWEET POTATOES

5 large yams
2 tablespoons butter or margarine
1 tablespoon grated orange peel

3 medium oranges
1/4 teaspoon salt
3/4 cup dark corn syrup

Cook yams in skins until fork tender. Peel and halve. Peel oranges, slice cross-wise. Combine butter, orange peel, syrup, and salt, heat to a boil. Pour over yams and oranges. Bake at 325° for 35 to 40 minutes.

BRUSSELS SPROUTS

1 pkg. frozen brussel sprouts
1/4 cup grated Parmesan cheese

1/2 stick butter
1 cup beef broth

Cook sprouts in broth. <u>Do not overcook</u>. Melt butter or margarine in saucepan, add sprouts, heat a few seconds in butter to which you have added Parmesan cheese. Serve at once.

Do not put lemon juice on green vegetables until just ready to serve.

LEMON CHEESE SAUCE

Combine 1 can (11 oz.) condensed cheddar cheese soup, 1/2 cup sour cream, 1 cup grated swiss cheese, 1 teaspoon grated lemon peel and 1 tablespoon fresh lemon juice in a saucepan. Heat, stirring until cheese melts. Serve over cooked broccoli or asparagus.

CUCUMBERS IN SOUR CREAM

3 cucumbers, sliced
1 onion, sliced into rings
1 teaspoon garlic salt
1 tablespoon chives
paprika

1/4 teaspoon salt
1/2 pint sour cream
1/2 teaspoon wine vinegar
fresh green pepper

Soak cucumbers and onion overnight in ice water and salt. Drain thoroughly. combine remaining ingredients except paprika and pour over cucumber and onions. Mix thoroughly and sprinkle with paprika. Serves 6 or more.

STUFFED PEPPERS

6 green or red bell peppers
2 tomatoes
2 cups rice (cooked) or corn
1 1/2 cups ham cooked and ground

1 onion
4 ribs celery
2 tablespoons butter

Cut off stem ends of peppers, remove seeds. Chop ends of peppers, the celery and onion; fry in butter or margarine until tender. Add chopped tomatoes, cook until soft, add rice and ham, cook until most of the moisture has absorbed. Stuff mixture in peppers, put buttered crumbs on top. Put in pan with a little hot water. Bake at 350° for 10-15 minutes. (You can use ground beef in this.) (If you prefer, you can parboil peppers for a few minutes before stuffing.)

FRENCH FRIED ONIONS

1 cup plain flour
1/4 teaspoon salt
1 egg white, beaten
large Bermuda onions

1 tablespoon salad oil
2/3 cup water
sweetened ice water

Cut the onions in halves cross-wise. Slice 1/8 inch thick, using only large middle slices. Separate rings and cover with sweetened ice water (about 1 heaping tablespoon of sugar to a bowl of water). Leave onion rings in ice water for 2 hours. Drain thoroughly and wipe dry. Combine ingredients for batter, beating until smooth. Add oil and fold in beaten egg white. Dip each ring in the batter and fry in deep hot fat to a delicate brown. Drain on paper towels. Sprinkle with salt. (These are always crisp and delicious. This batter is also good for frying other vegetables and is even good for shrimp.) (This recipe came from an old Louisiana cook book.)

MIXED VEGETABLES

2 boxes of frozen lima beans
2 boxes of frozen green peas
2 boxes of frozen green beans

Cook peas, limas, and green beans until done. Drain. Set aside and keep warm.

Sauce:
2 cups mayonnaise
1 tablespoon Worcestershire sauce
1 teaspoon prepared mustard
4 hard-cooked eggs, sieved

4 tablespoons oil
dash of Tabasco
grated onion to taste

Mix all ingredients together and when ready to serve, pour sauce over vegetables. (You can also serve this cold as a salad.)

Ransen - Pomarede

PICKLES, RELISHES AND PRESERVES

CRANBERRY APRICOT CONSERVE

1 pkg. cranberries (1 lb.)
2 cups orange juice
1/2 cup water

1 lb. dried apricots
1 1/4 cups sugar

Stir all ingredients together in large saucepan and let boil for 5 or 6 minutes. Turn down heat and simmer for 30 minutes. Keeps for weeks in refrigerator. (Luscious!)

SQUASH PICKLE

8 cups sliced squash (yellow)
3 cups sliced green bell pepper

2 cups sliced onions

Cover above ingredients with water with:

1/3 cup pickling salt added.

Soak for 1 hour and drain.

3 cups sugar
2 teaspoons celery seed

2 cups vinegar
2 teaspoons mustard seed

Bring these ingredients to a boil. Add squash, onions, and peppers. Boil for 3 minutes. Can in hot, sterile jars and seal. (Tastes like bread and butter pickles.)

MIXED PICKLE

2 quarts chopped green tomatoes
1 quart chopped red tomatoes
1 medium cabbage, chopped
4 green sweet peppers, chopped
4 red sweet peppers, chopped
4 large onions, chopped
1 cucumber, chopped

Sprinkle 1/2 cup pickling salt over all and let stand overnight. Drain.

2 stalks celery, chopped
1 teaspoon ginger
1 tablespoon white mustard seed

3 pints vinegar
3 lbs. sugar (6 cups)
1 tablespoon dry mustard

Mix these ingredients with drained vegetables and cook until clear, slowly. Put in hot, sterile pint jars. Makes about 8 pints. (This is a delicious, mixed pickle.)

ZESTY RELISH

2 medium turnips, pared and cut up
1/2 medium onion, chopped
1 tablespoon prepared horseradish

1/4 cup vinegar
1/2 teaspoon salt
1 1/2 tablespoons sugar

Put all ingredients in blender and mix. Serve on turnip greens or other vegetables. Will keep in refrigerator for several days.

EASY CRANBERRY SAUCE

Put 1 (1 lb.) bag cranberries in a 9 x 13 inch pan. Sprinkle with 1 cup sugar. Cover pan with foil and bake in a 275° oven for 1 hour. Cranberries will pop and sizzle, but do not remove foil. Let continue baking for the 1 hour. Then uncover and mix 1/2 jar of orange marmalade with hot cranberries.

SPICED FRUIT

Simmer 1/2 cup honey, 1 cup orange juice, 1/2 teaspoon allspice, 1/2 teaspoon cinnamon, and a dash of salt.

Pour this over chopped fruit (pineapple, bananas, apples, grapes or any fruit). Just before serving pour a small amount of lemon lime soda over each serving. Use 7-up, Sun Drop, or Mello-Yello. (Refreshing)

CRANBERRY RELISH

1 bag cranberries (1 lb.)
2 oranges, pulp and some rind chopped fine
2 ribs celery
1 teaspoon lemon juice
1 1/4 to 1 1/2 cups sugar (depending on sweetness of oranges)
1/2 cup chopped pecans

Grind or chop all ingredients in food processor. Add sugar and nuts and stir well. Refrigerate for at least 24 hours before eating. Keeps well for weeks in refrigerator. (This is the most delicious cranberry relish you ever tasted.)

PEPPER RELISH

1 dozen red sweet peppers   *3 hot peppers*
1 dozen green sweet peppers   *4 onions*
2 cups sugar   *1 quart vinegar*
3 tablespoons pickling salt

Grind peppers and onions and pour boiling water over them. Let stand for 5 minutes. Pour off and put on more boiling water. Let stand for 5 minutes. Then pour off water and put in large deep vessel with sugar, salt, and vinegar and cook until tender. Seal while hot in hot, sterile jars. (This is an old recipe and so good on vegetables or hamburgers.)

PEPPER JELLY

1 1/2 cups ground bell green peppers (can use some red ones)
1 long pod hot pepper (ground)
1 1/2 cups cider vinegar
1 bottle Certo
6 1/2 cups sugar

Mix peppers, sugar and vinegar and bring to a boil. Boil hard for 2 minutes. Take off heat and add Certo, stirring well. Pour into small sterile jars. (This is delicious with meat or on crackers mixed with cream cheese.)

CRISP GREEN TOMATO PICKLE

7 lbs. green tomatoes
3 cups lime

Cut tomatoes in slices and soak in 2 gallons water with lime for 12 hours. Wash off thoroughly and soak in clear water for 3 hours. Drain.

Syrup:
  5 lbs. sugar   *3 quarts vinegar*
  2 teaspoon whole cloves   *1 teaspoon allspice*
  1 teaspoon powdered ginger   *1 teaspoon celery seed*

Mix and let come to a boil then pour over tomatoes. Let stand overnight. Cook for 1 hour, then seal in hot, sterile jars. Makes 5 quarts or 10 pints.

BREAD AND BUTTER PICKLES

Slice thin 12 medium size cucumbers   6 small onions, sliced
Soak for 2 hours in 1/2 cup coarse plain salt, water to cover. Add ice.

Boil for 1 minute: 2 cups sugar, 2 cups apple cider vinegar, 1 teaspoon each of ginger, celery seed, tumeric, 2 teaspoons mustard seed, 1 teaspoon cornstarch. Add drained cucumbers and onions and heat. Put in hot, sterile jars. Makes 4 pints.

HYDEN SALAD PICKLE

1 gallon ripe tomatoes (measured after chopping)
1 quart onions (chopped)
1 gallon cabbage (measured after chopping)
10 green peppers (chopped)   *1 bunch celery (chopped)*
6 cups sugar   *2/3 cup pickling salt*
1/2 gallon vinegar   *2 tablespoons tumeric*
1 tablespoon each of ginger, cloves, dry mustard, and cinnamon

Chop vegetables (can use food processor being careful not to chop too fine). Mix with salt and let drain for 2 hours (I use an old pillow case and let drain in sink). Mix spices, sugar, and vinegar with drained vegetables and cook slowly for 1 hour. Makes 10 or 11 pints. (This is the tastiest, best pickle! So good with hamburgers or vegetables.)

EASY CRISP SWEET PICKLE

2 tablespoons alum powder
1 gallon sour pickles (store bought)(not sliced)
5 lbs. white sugar
1 box pickling spice
1 bunch garlic buds
1 cup cider vinegar
1/2 cup tarragon vinegar

Drain pickles well and throw away juice. Do not use vinegar that comes in the jar of pickles. Slice pickles 1/4 inch thick and soak in ice water with alum powder for 2 hours, add ice often to keep pickle cold. Drain and rinse. In large crock jar pour 1 inch of sugar, 1 inch of sliced pickle, sprinkle with pickling spice and add several pieces of garlic. Repeat this process until all pickles and other ingredients have been used. Pour both vinegars over top and let stand 48 hours, stirring occasionally. Put pickles into hot, sterile jars but remove most of garlic. Makes 10 pints. (This pickles is every bit as good as pickle made by a long process.)

LIME PICKLES

2 gallons sliced cucumbers
2 cups lime in warm water to cover cucumbers.

Let stand overnight. Rinse and let stand in ice cold water. Drain

4 pints vinegar
1/2 box pickling spice (tied in bag)

4 lbs. sugar (8 cups)
2 teaspoons salt (not iodized)

Mix all ingredients and put in cucumbers. Simmer in mixture for 2 hours or boil for 1 hour. Put in sterile jars. (Crisp and good)

PEAR RELISH

3 quarts of chopped pears
3 1/2 lbs. onions, chopped
8 green bell peppers, chopped
1 tablespoon celery seed
1 tablespoon white mustard seed
3 or 4 hot peppers, chopped

1 quart vinegar
3 cups sugar
3 tablespoons pickling salt
1 tablespoon tumeric

Mix all ingredients together. Boil for 15 minutes. Seal in hot, sterile jars.

SWEET PEACH PICKLE

7 lbs. fruit
4 lbs. (8 cups) sugar
1 tablespoon whole allspice
1 tablespoon stick cinnamon (broken)

1 pint vinegar
1 pint water
1 tablespoon whole mace
1 tablespoon whole cloves

Tie spices in cheesecloth bag. Make syrup of sugar, vinegar, water, and spices. Boil about 10 minutes. Drop peeled peaches in syrup. Cook until tender. Take peaches out and pack in hot, sterile jars. Boil syrup about 10 minutes longer. Pour over peaches and seal. (Delicious with meats.)

PICKLED OKRA

4 lbs. small tender okra
3/4 cup plain (not iodized) salt
10 pods red or green hot peppers

1 cup water
8 cups pure vinegar
10 cloves garlic

Wash okra. Be sure pods are small, leaving short stem of pod. Pack in hot, clean jars. Place 1 pepper pod and 1 clove of garlic in each jar. Heat vinegar, water and salt to boiling. Pour hot vinegar over okra and seal. Let stand for 8 weeks before using. Makes 10 pints.

RHUBARB JAM

5 cups rhubarb, diced
4 cups sugar
1 small can crushed pineapple
1 (3 oz.) box strawberry jello

Mix sugar and rhubarb. Let set 30 or 40 minutes. Add pineapple and cook for 30 minutes. Add jello, stirring until dissolved and thick. Put into sterile jars.

PEACH CONSERVE

3 lbs. peaches
2 small bottle maraschino cherries
1 (8 1/4 oz.) can crushed pineapple,
   not drained

2 oranges
3 lbs. sugar
1/2 teaspoon salt

Peel and chop peaches, add oranges that have been sliced thin, peel and all. Add cherry juice, sugar, salt, 2 or 3 peach seeds. Boil hard for 30 minutes. Stir often. Add cherries, cut in rings and pineapple. Continue cooking until thick, about 25 minutes. Spoon into hot, sterile jars. Let set overnight. Seal. Put in freezer if desired, but will keep out of freezer. (Nice to put in small jars for gifts.)

CRYSTAL CRUNCH PICKLE

7 lbs. fully mature cucumbers

Measure after peeling and cutting out sides and cutting into sticks. Put 2 cups lime and enough water to cover cucumbers and let stand for 24 hours. Second day, rinse well, put in 4 oz. alum and enough water to cover well. Let set 6 hours. Rinse, put in clear, ice cold water and let stand for six hours. Drain.

2 1/2 quarts white vinegar   *14 cups sugar*
2 1/2 quarts water   *1 tablespoon pickling salt*
3 tablespoons pickling spice   *1 tablespoon celery seed*

Bring this mixture to a boil after pouring over cucumbers. Take off and let set overnight. Put on stove and cook until sticks are transparent. Pack in hot sterile jars. (Nice to serve on a party place.)

REFRIGERATOR PICKLES

6 cups sliced cucumbers, 3/8 inch thick
1 cup sliced onion
1 cup green pepper, sliced
2 cups sugar
1 cup vinegar
1 tablespoon celery seed
2 tablespoons salt (not iodized)

Let sliced vegetables drain in a colander for two hours. Bring sugar, vinegar, celery seed, and salt to a boil. Let cool. Pour over vegetables in a large bowl; mix well. Place in jars or plastic containers with tight lid. Keeps in refridgerator indefinetely. (Easy and good to have on hand.)

Ramsey. Pomarede

Index

AFTERWORD

In 1938, Bob Ramsey married Ida Shelton Taylor. She was a twenty-one-year-old Southern girl, and he was a twenty-seven-year-old farm boy with a degree from Georgia Tech in Civil Engineering. They were in love in 1938, and they are still in love in 1994.

Love does not conquer everything, though. As a farm boy, Bob was accustomed to eating hearty meals, especially breakfast. Ida's Mississippi Delta upbringing had spoiled her with the luxury of servants who cooked all of the family meals. There were no servants to cook for Bob and Ida in their new Tennessee home. Thus, there was a problem — Ida couldn't cook.

As legend has it, the problem was manifested ... and cured ... at breakfast one morning. Ida could only cook toast for breakfast — not eggs, not bacon, not biscuits, not grits — nothing else. After suffering several mornings of this low calorie, low cholesterol breakfast, Bob dryly commented, as only he could, "Man does not live by bread alone." This comment was not an effort to initiate a religious discussion with his new wife, but rather a subtle complaint about the lack of breakfast substance.

The effect on Ida was greater than that intended. First, she cried for days. But then, in keeping with her incredibly strong character, she vowed to learn to cook. And learn she did. As demonstrated by this cookbook and several others she has authored, she is now a world-class cook.

By the time, I, Bob and Ida's youngest son came along, she had honed her skill to near perfection. I have many fond memories of my childhood, and of my loving parents and family; several of them center around one of Mama's fabulous meals.

As an expression of my love and admiration for my beloved Mother and Father, I have assisted in the preparation, publishing and printing of this cookbook. I sincerely hope that each of you that use and read this book will feel and understand even a smidgen of the pride and emotion I will always feel when I hear the words "Ida's In The Kitchen."

Bill Ramsey

Ida's Love And Ida's Kitchen

We, who shared, celebrate Ida's book
Of food; when young we leapt
Upon her crusted bread, siphoned
Her ice cream like thieves.

So, Ida's children, and I,
Now hold high a stem of grain
In our palms and recall the fruit
Of our young and nurtured lives.

Each may invoke a scene:
Me, Ida's water-beaded hands
In the kitchen sun, moving bread;
Bread to oven and kids to door.

And we would go, build our raft,
Play football, or explore for old coins;
Our realm of youth having the comfort
Of Ida's love and Ida's kitchen.

Now, in our years we have felt the full sun,
And fruit and grain in season.
Our realm of youth having the comfort
Of Ida's love and Ida's kitchen.

So we, Bobby, Betty, Bill ... and I
Pledge high a glass and a shoot of grain
To toast our realm of youth and the comfort
Of Ida's love and Ida's kitchen.

Mike Galligan